Introduction

A healthcare marketer for over 16 years. Has diverse experience in corporate communications, digital marketing, sales, strategic implementations, international inbound medical tourism, and business development.

She loves and appreciates creativity. Can Sketch, Sing (for herself), and somewhat play guitar frets. She is different around different people, so some call her stubborn, and others call her jovial.

She loves to communicate her heart out to people who she vibes with and keeps it short and simple with others. Sometimes curt ;) as she likes to be real; she cannot fake at all but tries to be politically correct.

An observer, who likes to keep the details to herself, though she talks unapologetically with the closest pals. Likes to improve each day and yet sometimes is very critical of self.

A Gemini who is yet to find answers to a lot of questions and would never look for them outside of her.

She sees the world differently, sometimes in 3D without her being part of it. Meditates, to search what lies within her, which continues with self-talk before she starts her day.

Jagruti Mistry

SILENTLY

....my mind

NOISY

....minds speaking

JAGRUTI MISTRY

First Published in December 2021

ISBN: 978-93-5472-848-8

BLUEROSE PUBLISHERS
www.bluerosepublishers.com
info@bluerosepublishers.com
+91 8882 898 898

Cover Design:
Geetika Kandari

Typographic Design:
Namrata

Distributed by: BlueRose, Amazon, Flipkart

Dedication

To my parents Pushpa Mistry and Ramchandra Mistry, I wouldn't have been inspired to do what I wanted to do without their support. My mom in particular who trusts me blindly and that's what always gives me the confidence of stepping into the new.

Contents

1. Understanding Self:

Full of thoughts, emotions, inspiration, positivity, dreams, negativity, laziness we're all different. We enjoy socializing as we like knowing everyone who is different from us, yet we try to find a similarity between each other. So simple yet so complicated.

We love to live in our heads and find answers which just satisfy our perceptions. It's difficult most of the time to understand the other side of the story or a different perspective. Ever wondered what happens to us while we grow up?!

A child is not influenced by any external thinking, decisions, and therefore experiments and sees everything differently. We, on the other hand, are worried so much about the opinions of others, that we build our personalities around their expectations.

The world may seem unreal because somewhere, so are we, only a few people may get a glimpse of who we exactly are.

Everyone was always previously masked (even before COVID-19); we would all be surprised if minds could talk loudly, the opinions and thoughts would have startled us. Today, I think we are getting more towards awareness, of who we are and what needs to be done.

So what needs to change?

- *A good Self-talk, to understand yourself*
- *To think before we speak*

- *To be empathic towards others*
- *To treat everyone with compassion*
- *To be honest in our speech, by honest I don't mean rude. but to subtly be able to convey the truth*
- *To be more in the other person's shoes while listening or talking, that's when we will be able to reply with appropriate answers or create a meaningful conversation.*

2. Horizon is an illusion –

Horizon is a beautiful illusion, what we see is not what it exactly is.

But, if it seems good to your mind, then it would be better not to get to the detail.

Similarly, we sometimes get too much into detail of situations so much so, the beauty and the purpose of a situation are lost. In general, it's not important to scrutinize life, the deeper you think the different your answers would get.

What we always need to do is make peace with the situation and let go. If you let go, you won't wander. There are newer chapters ahead, there are newer memories to build, there are newer battles to be won.

Carrying on and moving on every time is much better than dwelling in the past.

3. It's all about YOU

It's important! Your definition of yourself is important. What you feel about yourself is important. What you think is important… You are your priority, even an aircraft asks you to put your oxygen mask first and then to help the person sitting beside you.

Always have 2 brief positive descriptions about yourself:

The first one needs to be for your present self and the second one needs to be for who you want to become. A lot of your inspiration comes from your surroundings and that's what you become.

Will you always want to be inspired by others? Or would you like to become an inspiration?

The second one is as important as the first. Yes, we do have role models, but we always need to find our own "new self" to become someone's role model.

It is important to check what our routine comprises. Are we dragging our day by merely able to complete the firefighting work? Or is our day well planned? **TIME** is the most precious commodity which needs to be valuated and evaluated.

Think about this! So, we know our birthday right? Had we known our last day on earth, would we function the way we function today?

Take each day as a box of chocolates every second one chocolate will disappear. Will you now choose the best chocolate to be eaten and prioritize?

Prioritize your day and make a list of things you need to complete during the day, unimportant and less urgent stuff can wait.

Our experiences are a compilation of our work that we do each day. Make your experience count!

4. Mind over Matter

Everyday hundreds and thousands of thoughts run through our minds. How does one focus despite having so much to think about?? Well, no one ever taught us how to shut our minds, because maybe it is required to be always at work. Our eyes on the other hand when closed, can relax.

It's not in our control to stop our minds from working incessantly; however, it is definitely in our control to channelize those thoughts. It is possible to re-wire a mind, I don't mean surgically, but we can work on the way it thinks, what it thinks, and whenever possible to re-direct thoughts from wandering.

Negativity is addictive, people more often like to be surrounded and clutter their minds with negativity. When surrounded by negative, you feel so low that you don't want to do anything. This is one reason for finding excuses for not doing anything and thinking unnecessarily. Negativity gets people into the comfort zone of not wanting to push themselves: 1. To move out of the situation and 2. To do what they are supposed to do otherwise.

Though people are fully aware of what is required to be done, they just refuse to shift their focus to the task at hand.

Positivity is a choice, when practiced over a period it becomes a lifestyle. They say, getting motivation is like having a bath, must be a daily habit. If you fail to keep yourself motivated, a lot of calcification of negativity gets in the way of your progress. A positive attitude goes a long way in helping oneself and most importantly helping people around us.

Things change around you when you choose to change, and the results definitely change.

It's, therefore, mind over matter, if you don't mind it doesn't matter, whatever the external situation is Positivity will be your second nature, the first one, of course, will be your habits!

5. Don't Charge yourself of what goes wrong... Be in charge...

Being in charge means being aware of what you do. Often people go by their day as it comes. It is good to be accepting of what's ahead of you, but it is certainly not appropriate to not plan it at all.

Take time to be just by yourself and go through your day in your head before you go through it in real. Sounds weird? It isn't actually, most of the time (in fact, all the time) when you go through all your "to do's" during the day you kind of play the entire situation in your head first, this is called visualization. It works miraculously. Studies say that if you can visualize what you want, and you can feel the emotion of being in that space of achievement, then you will be the master of yourself and your life.

Did I deviate from the actual subject? mmm, I guess no. This should be a part of your routine, that's how you will be able to be in the driver's seat of your life, rather than being like driftwood and have external sources control you.

When you start practicing small good changes in your routine, you will achieve a slightly changed version of yourself in due course. Your close ones will certainly notice this change. This change is called Discipline.

Discipline is one of the first few things, which is taught in school. I don't know how many of us remember. Right from getting up early, dressing up for school neat and tidy, eating lunch from the respective tiffin boxes, reciting prayers well, and Ohh! the queue that you were made to stand in (the shortest first and the tallest last).

Somewhere, people stop upgrading the list of disciplines that one needs to have over time. The more you grow in independence, the more you get accustomed to the so-called "breaking the rules" mindset. Of course, you can let yourselves loose, but not to an extent of becoming intractable.

If everyone chooses to be a better self and be in control of their life, it will not take time to change things around you.

Discipline builds character and change upgrades not only you but everyone around you...

6. Zid! (Hindi) How stubborn are you?-

Being Stubborn may not always be bad. I like the word **Zid** more, sounds more impactful. "*Zid ho toh kuch bhi haasil kar sakte ho*" this is a saying in Hindi, which means, if you are stubborn enough to achieve your dreams, anything else doesn't matter- neither your education nor your background or even your bank balance.

The question is how one finds this quality in oneself and build it so strongly that it helps you chase your goals, even at your lowest motivated self.

Everyone has their kind of favorite thing to do, which is their stress buster; be it playing a musical instrument, sketching, dancing, etc. I have seen some software developers who aren't so into their respective profiles at work, but love to develop fun applications in their 'me time'. This could be your game-changer, the more you stimulate your brain to work on what you love to do the most; you will have more ideas on making it your mainstream work. It may be your IKIGAI (having a direction or purpose in life).

The problem is, do we take ourselves seriously? Well, doesn't mean we need to get all serious. What I am trying to address here is, that we often are unaware of what is that one thing which we are good at. There may also be more than one talent that each one of us possesses. But, have we identified it yet? For example, A person may be good at sketching, when one starts following what one loves, there is an immense focus that is happening unknowingly, it's like meditation to your brain.

If you pursue what you like to do and make it your living, you will never work a day in your life. What happens is, education and then our respective professions make life so monotonous that we park our passion and completely forget about it. Then when suddenly someone asks us what we like doing, we have to think hard.

Of course! Career is important but, are we pausing to check on ourselves or are we just living a routine which is wink passing. Think about it!

7. How you see the world, and how the world sees you...

Do you know, you're wearing binoculars all the time? The binoculars of judgment, you are judging almost everything all the time and, you have your respective opinion on everything. Mostly you do not vocalize it, but you build on it.

You have a perception of everyone's nature as well, that person may not essentially be the way you think he/she is and that is exactly why you get along with some people and may not with few others.

At times, there may have been instances of best friends suddenly parting ways, or couples after having a very strong marriage for decades get separated or there may be differences within the families. What goes wrong here?

The answer is Situations!!! Situations make us react differently.

Everyone reacts differently to different situations. If two people or groups are not able to accept those reactions or responses, that's when judgment starts building up. **Negative judgment is capable of building distances.**

You cannot change the reaction of the other person in a situation, but you certainly can control your reaction to it. There's a quote I read somewhere; "10 percent of the conflicts happen due to differences in opinion and rest 90 percent, due to use of the wrong tone in the voice". I am totally in agreement with this phrase. A disagreement or an argument won't end unless one stops reacting to it. If you don't react you won't get a response, simple!

On the other hand, you feel way too offended when you are being judged, right? You would get defensive or more so, you would conclude that the person is being judgemental. You need to understand, If you don't like to be judged, you should not be doing the same to others as well. Yes, everyone has a first draft of their opinion about someone, but that's the first draft, rather, it should be a first draft for everyone to go back and rectify what needs to be changed for better.

How I wish the world would be without judgment.

Imagine if the adjectives you used for judging people were imprinted like tattoos on your skin, what would you want to be written on your own body??? Would you still judge, is the question?

8. When He and She struggle to express

His point of view

He is a guy who is scared to be in a relationship because of his conservative family. Times have changed and yet he thinks what his parents would say if he dated a girl, who is not the way his family pictured. His family has already quoted him a perfect detail of a girl they want as their daughter — in — law (even the profession). Therefore, here he is, telling himself **"No, I won't date anyone yet, not even if I come across someone"**.

But there is something else planned for him. He meets someone at his workplace, he unexpectedly gets into the first-ever conversation with her which lasts for an hour. Not that the conversation was an interesting one, but the people in the conversation find each other interesting (I guess because the conversation certainly wasn't that engaging).

They meet every day in office, brief conversations turn into morning coffee and evening snack meetings. Before he realizes, he slips into a habit of wanting her always around. Sharing everything with her that he has never previously expressed to anyone becomes his regime. He is so overly affectionate about her that at times he would just hold on to a call to hear her fall asleep. Still, he'd claim that "we're friends okay".

Time goes by, but he stops himself from thinking if this is anything more than just friendship. No, wait! Let me reframe. He knows that he loves her, but he doesn't want to express, because remember his family who has an ideal picture? She did not fit that picture perfectly. So, he tags her as a friend and makes peace with his heart and mind.

Life goes on for him. But here's a thing.

We don't sometimes get what we want, but life certainly gives you what you deserve. In this case, he had a choice of changing the result, however, though, his priority here was different. He may not be wrong, but neither was she.

Her point of view

She is the kind of girl who does not get into any relationship without being sure. She meets this guy of course in the same office. But, as "he" recollects of their first conversation in person, she fondly remembers their first conversation on a call, which was incidental (not accidental). She gets impressed by the intellect and later when she meets him in person for a professional conversation, she wants to speak more. He doesn't realize that she had driven the conversation for an hour. Interesting! Haahaa.

Of course, both have a lovely conversation. Not realizing the swirl that the conversation had created. She goes by the days ahead casually because the kind of person she is, she just loves conversations.

So, since she'd had her share of good conversation, it was conveniently forgotten, and neither did she continue or keep up the momentum in their subsequent meetings. But this time she doesn't realize that he was making an effort to communicate.

Her then colleague now friend, discovers that there seems to be a vibe that he is trying to pass and that he may be interested in pursuing this ahead. As surprised (but pleasantly) that she is, she doesn't want to believe initially, but as she starts noticing she understands.

Now, because she is coy and ambivalent at the same time, she takes a few steps back and reduces the communication between them. She wants to know if it's serious, because of course *"No casual relations"*.

Yes, time goes by here as well. But somewhere, she does realize that she hasn't made any effort to like someone else either, maybe because she has started liking him.

So, she waits.. waits.. waits and waits because she wants him to initiate. But, with no luck, she gives up and decides to speak and expresses her heart out. Sadly, because of his reasons (peer pressure) he chooses to keep quiet initially, neither a yes nor a no. She gets downhearted seeing him explaining his side, clearly denying any feelings for her in the first place. Therefore, she chooses to end the conversation asking him to stop justifying.

In this case, somewhere she knew that this may not work out, but she only gave him time because she loved genuinely and refused to give up. She neither regrets the time she had with him nor does she regret being without him now. Because she does realize she met him for a reason, and that whatever they had as friends was spent well.

Of course, she did feel bad, but that was momentary and nothing compared to what she experienced when they were together.

However, the best decision she took was to choose not to be in touch and refrain from any communication ahead because being friends again would have devalued the importance and presence of this person in her life.

Some people come in your life to teach you lessons that are meant for your growth; and there's this someone who breeze passes you, only to leave an imprint in your heart that you carry for the rest of your life.

9. Perspective anyone?

"Perspective"- A term that is more often used in today's time to describe one's opinion or a point of view on something. Where does it come from?

You are loaded with tonnes of information every single day, which you keep consuming knowingly and sometimes unknowingly. What you derive out of that information becomes your "so-called perspective" or opinion towards that subject.

Most of your thought processes are built right from your childhood, where you are taught to believe in a specific manner. It takes years of programming of the brain to build the way you think or operate. Your personality is made up of everything that you have known, learned, and implemented so far. Let's call yourself a seed that gets the first nourishment from the soil, the role of soil in your life is played by your parents. And, then the further watering to this sapling is done by your friends, relatives, colleagues, and people that are around.

On average you are a combination of thoughts comprised of the people around you. Ever wondered when your circle of people changes why does it take you time to connect with them and adapt to the way they communicate or the topics that they strike in their routine communication?

Because those are their set of perspectives, somewhere you wouldn't find them relatable.

Do you make an effort to re-visit your opinions? As any program can get obsolete and would require a Version 2.0; you also need to re-wire the way you think. Sometimes, it is a good thought to give another perspective a chance. Maybe, just maybe, you get a better version of your opinion.

Improvising is the key, your thoughts and opinions may be good however, everything has a scope of improvement.

So, when you think of arguing on a point of view, hold back for just a few seconds before you reply. I remember a quote that says- "You need to understand first, and then want to be understood".

10. You are always in the right place at the right time. Period!

Ever occurred to you that your life may be planned? Certain instances happen which just change the direction and the course of your life.

You may be best friends with people whom you have met only briefly and get along so well, that they become an inseparable part of your life. Billions of people in the world, over hundreds of countries, and yet you meet these specific people; learn from them, understand them, and eventually end up knowing just them among the rest of the world.

These I feel are chosen ones, just for you. And so is your life, specific to you, each of you has a different story, a story that is unique in its way. Yet, you take your story so casually and barely live it. Most of you; are interested in someone else's story, without even knowing, if you even fit the part.

The most important thing I want to address here is that you need to enjoy what you are brought to. But you are so busy analyzing it, that you've been missing the fun of being aware of what you are going through every single moment of every new day.

For Example, A person who has just passed out of college is trying to figure out the career. In the run, goes through 25 -30 rejections during the job search. Disheartened, questions the potential, cribs about not getting selected, but continues the job search just because there's no choice. Finally, gets selected in one of the most renowned firms one can ever dream to start a career with.

After a few years while going through a flashback of events, realizes that those rejections brought the person to this day. Because there were a few key links, that were related to the previous rejections which made complete sense to his current situation.

Whatever happens in your life, is necessary for you to move to the next level, anything different would take you to a completely different destination. One needs to be aware and grateful for all the instances that one is a part of until today. You are here in your present because of your past, therefore being aware of your present will create a better future.

So, here's a thing, at the end of each day go through your day, write one instance that was the best thing that happened that day, and be thankful. In a year, you will have a book full of instances and experiences to thank for. I am sure you will have a pleasant smile on your face every new year.

Keeping your resolutions will be easy that way ;)

11. Infinite possibilities. yet our minds are blindfolded

Everyone today is rising to the fact that thoughts are powerful. Your current situation is exactly the manifestation of what you have been thinking and manifesting till-date. Therefore, to change something, you need to change the way you think.

You may have heard of a saying "What you sow, so shall you reap". If you look around right now, everything around you has been a part of someone's manifestation of thoughts. Right from the device, through which you are reading my blog, to the couch/sofa/chair you are currently seated. Everything has been thought first and then has come into perspective. Who knew the robots that we enjoyed watching as cartoon characters would translate into hi-tech devices today, which perform serious tasks and with such accuracy that I guess no human can replace.

Your brain and heart have a mind of its own, which communicates, and that's why at sometimes you think you are in grave conflict with your heart and the mind.

Let's not get into the technicalities right now. You have no idea what doors can be opened if you tap into this unknown territory. I am not trying sound intellectual here, though I would like to ;)

On a serious note, you do have the power to change the results for yourself. It just requires you to focus on what you want rather than what is stopping you.

How many of you go according to your gut feeling? Some of us don't even bother listening to it. A gut feeling is an immediate feeling that you get seconds after you have seen, read, or heard something. Your gut already decides for you before-hand. Neither analysis nor logic is required but we have the capability of foreseeing something way in advance.

You need to understand yourself first, it's the most important thing to do. Look within before you look outside for answers. Even your stomach tells us what is palatable for us and what isn't. Each cell of our body has a mind of its own. So every time you make a decision, observe what your mind and heart are trying to communicate and then go accordingly without any disbelief and see changes happening all around you.

If we give in to it and practice knowing it more, we may get into a habit of making the right choices, at least most of the time.

12. No one can steal you from you... Be Unique

Everyone is unique in their way. One can be a first mover to do a lot of things, it only requires discovering oneself. The creator has been kind and creative enough to make you so uniquely different despite being quite similar in structure and being. Also, despite being unique, each one has limitless untapped potential. It may just take a certain amount of extra effort for an ordinary to be extra-ordinary. That one step is to discover your strengths and ignore the weakness.

If fishes were asked to fly and birds were asked to swim, they would lead their entire lives considering themselves good for nothing. It is therefore primarily important for an individual to discover what each is good at.

I think everyone should start early, in fact way too early. There should be a better way to educate children, apart from the routine academic syllabus. If there was a self-development time that was allotted in schools that allowed children to do whatever they wanted and explore ideas; like in an open forum where skills, craft, anything, and everything was introduced to them. so they could explore their minds and ideas freely.

Ideas are like a blueprint, if not implemented on time they become obsolete. Millions of ideas run through your minds every day, have you ever thought to explore even one of them so far? You never know, for the one you may have missed implementing, would have been a brilliant one.

You have strengths that may not be comparable to what your current focus area is, yet you are more concerned about what you cannot achieve rather than what you can.

Once you have discovered your strength, you can work on the overall self-alongside. Each day you need to be better than yesterday. Here, you are not competing with anyone, but you are bettering yourself than what you were yesterday.

Presently you are so occupied in your respective jobs, studies, and routine that all this while you have been upgrading your knowledge and skills according to the industry/career requirements. As a person, you may have not grown comparatively. Being best in your domain is good, but are you a better individual, is a question worth giving a thought.

13. What's your Purpose in Life?

Everyone is too busy heading nowhere, sometimes, with no time to pause. Is life so unimportant to not know your purpose? Why are we exactly here?

Routine is the most silent prisoner; you don't even realize that you get consumed in the swirl of it. Right now, unknowingly you are only feeding your necessity, there's absolutely no time to do something else. I read this quote somewhere "To live, is so startling that there's no time for anything else". But are we living or we barely know what life stands for

LIFE: **L**iving **I**n a (so-called) **F**ascinating **E**nvironment

OR

Let your **I**ndividuality **F**ind **E**legance

The choice is yours. You work in organizations which have their respective *Mission Statements*, but you are not aware of your mission/goal. Do you have a mission statement yet? If no, then sit yourself down and write one. Hollywood actor Will Smith has one, which is ***"The world has to be a better place because I was here"***

I also have mine :) which says, ***"Become famous, make a difference to lives, be a synonym to compassionate and relentlessly positive, because ordinary just lacks the 'ex'tra factor."*** I think that's not too much to ask for; somewhere I have started working towards it.

Though I don't know if I should believe in life after death, I would still prefer to live in the moment and therefore I ensure that I live this one to the fullest. One LIFE!

What if God asks you "So, how was heaven"? I don't want any regrets there :)

Ask yourself, if whatever you are doing today was exactly what you wanted to do! If the answer is "No" find what you want to do in life. I don't mean to tell you to completely stop what you are doing, but you need to identify what clicks a spark in you. Once you find that, you would realize what you have been missing and rest no one needs to tell you. You'd then find your way in spending most of your time doing just what you like.

Clarity is what you deserve in whatever you do, in whatever you aspire to be, and most of all; in whatever you believe

14. Communicating with "The Self" ...

Everyone likes to share their feelings by talking; human beings are social animals; they require communicating and that's how language was introduced.

Though communication need not be only external, sometimes you need to communicate internally. By internally I mean with self, you don't verbalize with yourself, and never do you have time to sit and observe your thoughts in detail and how you feel in your head.

If there is a feeling or a thought that is pestering, you don't go to the crux of the emotion. You only know what it is doing to you superficially. However, when you probe further on what caused that emotion in the first place, you'd discover that the reason is minuscule. Sometimes you tend to complicate things to a much larger extent than the situation itself.

You need to first understand and accept that every situation around you has a solution; and that there is an answer to every question. Most of the time, you are more focussed on getting into the right and the wrong then the actual solution. Solutions are situational and time-bound, a particular solution may not be apt for a similar situation that occurs at different times.

Example: A mother gives her crying child his favorite toy and he stops crying. Few months down the line that child may not stop crying if you give him the same toy, he is no more excited to see that toy. This time you need to find another solution to distract him from crying.

Similarly, you need to find your stimulus to keep you from negativity. I recently came across a different way of tackling a bothersome thought.

Whenever anything is bothering me to an extent that I am not able to change my focus to something else, then I write that thought down in as much detailed manner as possible. What happens when I do that? Well, when I describe the feeling on a piece of paper, book, or diary and give it a read, I find the problem silly, so much so that it loses its power of bothering me. Another thing that happens, is that I have now transferred the thought on to the paper, so my mind feels free and lighter, because there was a shift of negative energy from my mind to the paper. This helps me to concentrate on important tasks henceforth.

Self-talk is much required, no one knows you better than you. Also, you will never be able to lie to yourself. So always give yourself a pep talk and an ear that acts as a shoulder to lean on when things get too personal to share. Always be your first best friend.

And, of course, there will always be your close-set with whom you can share anything under the sun, with no questions asked; and with no scope of judgment ;)

15. "Feeling low", is not a good place to be...

How often do you say "I am feeling very low today". This phase visits the mind time and again and for some people, it becomes a part of their excuse to not do anything and cling on to the comfort of the pity party. Every day you have a choice, either to focus and get excited about what's in store ahead of you or to complain of your mood which is not up to the mark and carry on the negative vibe for the entire day.

There is always a reason for your untimely mood swing, and 90% of the time you know the actual reason but don't what to address it. Because guess what? You may just find a solution to get over with it. Most of the time, you want to be consumed by the emotion and lean on it just so you have a reason to be lazy.

Ask yourself if you are wasting time by being in that situation for too long.

Firstly, you need to accept the fact that something is bothering you and is not allowing you to focus. Secondly, you need to address the reason for yourself first, facing it is the best thing to do. Thirdly, evaluate why it is on your mind for that long, and find a solution.

There are two ways to look at it:

1. Have a problem — Yes — Is there a solution yet — Yes — Then apply the solution and move on with life.

2. Have a problem — Yes — Is there a solution yet — No — Then since you can't do anything about it, let time resolve it and forget about it or change your focus.

It is important to know what's the priority of the moment, trust me, you are the best judge, and you know it all. Be sincere and truthful to yourself. Everything else will fall in place.

Change your focus, and your mood will change. Unless you want to shift your energy, you will not be able to help yourself. It's okay sometimes to not be okay. But, ask yourself is it worth being in that space for too long. Gather yourself, dust yourself, get up, and get going. Be a self-motivator, you don't always need an external source to pick you up, you are very much capable of carrying your head on your shoulders.

Doesn't it feel nice to speak to people who are always happy and smiling? Whenever you are around them your vibe changes, you will always find them in the same high and will get the best advice and inspiration from them.

Don't you think others think that too, they too like being around happy souls? Are you working on your happy self?

Don't be dependent on someone for your happiness or your mood, be independent; and most of all be dependable, so you can be someone else's light. Carve your way of life...

16. R for "Respect your Relations"

Being born in India gives one thing in abundance and that's people. You are surrounded by lots n lots of people. Some also stay in joint families where the average people count in each household is from a minimum of 6 to a maximum of 10. Sounds crazy right, how does one deal with so many people?

It's not difficult to deal with people, of course, one needs to understand each one deeply, but if you make an effort it's simple. Everyone just needs and seeks Respect & Love. You would think, why did I place Respect before Love because only when you respect someone, loving a person becomes easy.

Wouldn't you like to be respected by others? Think about it. Go back to an instance where someone out of nowhere did something thoughtful and genuine, wouldn't you remember that instance. The moment I asked you to think about an instance, your mind went to that particular situation, why? Because somewhere you loved that gesture and it had been a feel-good moment for you.

Everyone deserves to be respected, including you. Sometimes, you go out of your way to be nice to people who are from your outer circle. But you forget those who deserve the most attention, these are your close ones; including your parents, siblings, best friends, spouse, and the ones who care for you. Just because you know you have a free hand with them, you take them for granted. Ever imagined your life without them, you would even hate the thought of it right?

Gestures are most important in making your relation strong. You very rarely appreciate the food that your mom prepares for you, and never do you think of returning that love by making her breakfast or dinner, just so she relaxes and has a break for that day. How many times have you mentioned to her with your excited voice that "the food was yummy mom". How many times have you thanked your best friend for just bearing with your nonsense for all these years and treated them specially for just being there through your thick and thin? Or ever randomly hugged your partner or the person who loves you for understanding your silly mood swings and managing them just the way you like. These are little things that go a long way.

Most of the time what you do is more important than what you say. It's easy for you to point out someone else's mistakes, but it's rather offensive if someone points out yours. Instead of playing the blame game go ahead and start thinking a notch up by correcting someone else's fault or goof-up, so the person notices what you did and self corrects next time onward.

Most of the time you fail to understand how much these little things mean to people, it may probably just make someone's day.

"I love you" can be said in one way but shown in multiple ways. Show the person how much you care by your tiny little gestures and he/she will comprehend your "I love you". Gestures are unspoken words which mean

much more than the said ones sometimes. *Although saying good things to people you love from time to time won't take any effort either.*

17. Are you operating technology or is the technology operating you...

Education took us from thumb impressions to signatures and technology took us back to thumb impressions, courtesy the biometric machine. Man invented technology to reduce the workload and now you find yourself helpless without it.

Technology advances are huge and numerous, but today let's talk about the gadgets that we use (mobile phones and laptops to be precise)

Do you remember birthdays without being reminded by various applications that you have on your phone? Or maybe remember the top 5 phone numbers of the closest people you love? If your answer is "yes" Good news! You are not consumed by technology yet ;)

Most of you feel handicapped sans mobile phones/laptops/tablets etc. You are so technology dependant that you cannot imagine your life without being around it. Somewhere the personal touch of being surrounded by physical beings has been missing.

Today, even festive greetings are shared by sending forwards. A new year wish starts by sending a forwarded image at the stroke of the midnight hour. Where, most of us refrain from wishing bang at midnight and try sending these greetings either before time or later the next day, just because they may get network congestion. That's how insensitive this gets...

We require emojis to express our feelings. The fun of enjoying life has been lost somewhere, everyone is so consumed in their respective routines that there is no time and space for emotions. Minds cannot focus because there is so much distraction around; the beeps and pings from the DM's, group messages, the Instagrams, and the Facebooks, so on and so forth.

To stop such distraction your mind compels you to switch off the devices or delete these apps from your phone. WHY? Can't you build so much muscle in your brain to change your focus from such distraction, instead of going to the extreme of deleting these applications from your phone? Are you so attached to technology, rather addicted that you can't merely move your focus to the more important tasks at hand?

Technology is supposed to be your strength, but you are moving towards making it your weakness. And that's completely losing the purpose of having it in the first place. You are on the path of becoming the slave to it, to an extent that when you hear a beep you go "Yes Master"!

Of course, one can have leisure time enjoying the World Wide Web and the gadgets one owns. But you need to know the limit to which you should spend time on it.

Research says that an average adult human brain has a capacity of storing data equivalent to approximately 2.5 million gigabytes of digital memory. You have a right to choose what you store and process in your beautifully designed brain.

Next time to get to know someone new, remember their birthday, and their phone number without depending on an application, you will be surprised that your brain can work wonders!

And, next time your phone beeps, think twice before you decide what deserves your focus more.

18. Read Yourself Before Others Read You

Have you heard someone say, I know you more than you know yourself. It's nice to have people around you who know you more than you do. But really! Is it not important to be aware of yourself first?

You have been with "you" all these years, you definitely know how you are, how you feel, how you react and certainly know your good and bad qualities. If you don't know, find out. You are representing yourself, you must be an impressive person to yourself first. I am not even talking about impressing others yet.

Impress yourself first, then the world.

Stop manipulating yourself by hiding your flaws; flaunt them instead, because they are yours and can be improvised. Accepting who you are is the first step towards self-love. You are the best and of course, you always have a scope for improvement. Never give up working on self.

Whenever you face a situation, you should know how to manage yourself first and then the situation. Everyone goes through ups and downs in life; good and bad days are part of everyone's lives. What matters is how one reacts to them.

No two individuals are the same and therefore would react differently to a similar situation.

You tend to often haste your reaction before understanding the scenario. And, most of the time after you have already reacted, you realize that there may have been a better way of handling it. But, by then it is too late.

So, there are people and there are people...

Some may never keep anything in their hearts and share everything with whom so ever they are comfortable, there are some, who are very vocal to everyone. Some people hold on to everything so close to their hearts that no one really knows what's going on. And then, some are super clear in what they think, act, and speak. Everyone is unique in their own way.

Let's talk about people who hold on to everything very close to their hearts and don't share at all; these are the ones who get hurt the most and very easily. But at the same time, these are the ones who behave like happy and carefree extroverts. Being secretive is one thing and swallowing your emotions is another. A lot of piling on happens which one day explodes like a volcano, and no one around you would ever know what happened.

A balance is required in everything, as much as one wants to keep things to themself, one needs to find a way to let go either by speaking to their close ones or writing it down in their journals. Because somewhere in the subconscious, it keeps affecting you. And, trust me you have no idea what it is causing you internally.

You are living in the world which fast-paced, there are very few people around you who genuinely care, what one needs to do is take everyone at the face value instead of reading into people and situations too much.

The more you dump your thoughts to an external source your mind lightens and you may cause less damage. Meditation is a good way to look within and be with yourself for those few minutes where you only focus on yourself. The better you know who you are and what you want the clearer you would get.

Treat yourself as your number one priority, learn everyday, improve everyday, introspect and know yourself better...

19. Human Nature Is Simple Yet Complex

In this entire so-called real world, everyone may not be 100 percent real. Also, the point here is are you real? So let's get this straight, people may be clear in life, but most of them have their secret side. Mostly, there may be people who to an extent of say 0.05 percent of the times are manipulating, I am not sure how good or bad this is. But this is precisely how certain people conduct themselves. Have you noticed this ever?

Now why does this happen, why aren't some of them real? The reason for each is it's own. Some are just trying to impress the external world around them. Some may be camouflaging their bad qualities. Some are trying to gel with the thought processes of people around them and some do that so others don't feel bad and for some; there may be absolutely no concrete reason.

Everyone has that secret side of themself which they don't want to show the world. But there are people in your life who may get a glimpse of this 'secretive 'nature of you. Those maybe your parents, your best buddy, your spouse, your siblings, basically; the ones who are very close to you.

Well, I am certainly not saying that you need not trust anyone. The point is that each requires introspection of how much does one need to keep things to themselves. You need to ask yourself a question, are you genuine? Being secretive doesn't really have to mean arrogance. It just means that the person may be slightly closed in expressing themself to the fullest. However, if one has a clear intent in whatever he/she does or communicates, then its fair for self and others. But, if someone manipulates his/her thoughts and speech every time around different people, that may not go well in long term relations.

Sometimes it is better to choose to keep quiet in a group or a conversation where you are not comfortable; instead of just playing along. This way, you wouldn't have to unnecessary lie or hide your discomfort.

Yes, some people are a little closed and don't want everyone to know them completely. These are the ones who genuinely need an ear to listen and a vibe to connect. Ensure that you have those close ones who know you inside out. That would enable you to express freely and sometimes break your inhibitions to an extent where you may come to terms with expressing yourself more freely.

People are complicated but if you genuinely vibe with someone, be true and trustworthy.

It takes a lot of effort to understand all aspects of a person's nature, and it's wonderful if you are able to read someone clearly and more fortunate to have someone who understands you completely. It's a small world, you may just meet around thousands of people, of all, you may only gel with a handful.

Enjoy knowing each other; it's fascinating to understand how each thinks, behaves, and reacts.

20. Vibe" is real!

All of you'll have experienced this, we all know that we have an energy aura which attracts and reflects. You meet so many people throughout, some you share a great bond, some become your close pals, some move on as you move on from your academic days to your career; or when you move from one job to another. But there are some handful of people who you instantly vibe with, when I say vibe it means there is this feeling that you know that person beforehand. You feel strange that you instantly get along with that person and start loving everything about that person instantly.

These are special people you should not let go, very rarely you find this feeling with people. These may be bonds which may convert to strong relationships if you really give it time. It may be a best friend bond, it may be a sibling bond, it may be a mentor and a disciple bond or it may be a partner bond.

It's very strange when you meet someone in the rarest of the scenario and that bond becomes the most awaited strongest bond ever in your life. Ever happened to you?

Today in the world which is mostly pretentious it is difficult to choose and trust people easily. Your minds are so used to the negativity around that everyone you like, the first thought that would cross your mind is what if the person is not worth the trust. However, the vibe that you get from someone will never fail you.

Trusting your inner voice is more important, however, situations will continue to happen though they should not stop you from doing what you think is right for that moment. Sometimes refraining from doing something you want will land you into regret later. So always, always do what you think is right. Trust your intuition and trust the vibe you get. It's not good to live in the judgement of your thoughts, because thoughts of misjudgement will do nothing well but only would crowd your mind with negativity. Release the judgement and keep it simple for yourself.

So always...

- Have a question? Ask

- Want to talk? Call

- Are you in two minds? Confront

- Thinking why did someone act differently? Express

- Not convinced with something? Discuss

Don't stop yourself from expressing what you feel, cuz when things don't go too well vibes get affected and that's when, a good, calm conversation can help you clear a lot of mental weight.

21. "Falling" in Love can be reframed to a better verb...

Falling in love, I really don't get why this has been an expression of someone who is in love. Well, falling represents hurt to me and I think it doesn't even go well with love. Let's just be in Love.

Right now when I am talking about love, all of you instantly had thought of that person who you are in love with presently. Didn't you? Don't lie okay!

Cuz I did too... It's amazing how someone has the capability to make you feel a million feelings in one thought. Your mood changes to whatever it was in the previous moment, to a happy mood and butterflies in your stomach. Isn't it great, to have someone in your life that has this effect on you?

But the point is why do people "fall out of love" because they did not love right in the first place? Or was it merely an infatuation?

There can be multiple reasons. Sometimes, circumstances make you end certain relationships. And these become unavoidable so much so even if you want to mend the relationship the situation takes over and your decision is more inclined towards ending it because you feel mending it will mean more compromises ahead.

For most of them, their first impression may be their last, though people who only get attracted to external factors like the looks, dressing sense so on, and so forth are the ones who's feelings sublime over a period of time. External beauty is perishable and so is love, if it's based on the same. So be aware of the kind of love you are into before you reach out to the person or express yourself. It's easy for everyone to get in and out of love but if that's what you want, then it will be very difficult for you to commit to anyone ahead.

People who have to move from one relationship to another for whatever their reason of moving on maybe, never really fall out of love with the previous person, they just love someone else more than they loved their previous partner. No one can completely forget their previous relations; however bad they were they may have always some good memories to cherish.

For some, it may just be a matter of going around and spending time with a person they just like to be with, it may not really involve a long commitment in their head or any futuristic plans with the person.

A lot of people may like to take this feeling for granted and therefore end up having so many wrong relations before they find the one. But in the run, what they don't realize is that they are teaching themselves to give up too easily and not adapt to the nature of the person.

Today, valuing a relation is rare, where so many couples are found to be parting ways, the primary reason for this may mostly revolve around not wanting to understand the other person. People are complicated, but you can always give an ear and ignore few fights just because your love for that person maybe a little more than the rest of the factors which can be overlooked.

Always be true and genuine to this valuable feeling that you have because it just makes you more humble more understanding and a different personality. Everyone likes to be loved. But when you are lucky to be the two of you who share mutual feelings for each other, then this bond becomes your strength and support. And most importantly it exposes you to your side which you did not come across previously.

22. Tone It Down

Everyone is full of expressions. You express, react, emote and that's how you are different from other living beings. You can convey so much better with the way you modulate your voice. Each one of you has a communicating style and somewhere that also defines a part of a person's nature.

But what you actually don't do is you don't listen to what you speak. Yes, I just said that. You only reply to respond not to convey what you feel.

Let me explain: When you respond it is basis your initial reaction and when you convey, it's more of a thoughtful reply. You may not want to respond the way you actually wanted to convey what you thought. And that's when you're in for an "uncalled for tiff".

Ever imagined what a tone of your voice can do to a situation or a relation. When you are in an argument, invariably the tone in your voice goes a couple of notches up, and that's not good for a conversation. Because, you not only go far from closure in the conversation, but also tend to spoil the mood of both involved. And most of the time once you are through with the argument, both of you regret the entire conversation. Few may also forget the reason for the fight. But the problem here is, words spoken and voice raised cannot be taken back, because the damage is already done.

Practicing not to react in the spur of the moment is the key to avoid such situations. Whenever your brain is ready to have your first reaction voiced, wait a couple of seconds before you speak. Your tone will be much controlled when you make yourself aware of your speech. The same sentence can mean differently if it's modulated well.

A simple sentence like: "Get me a glass of water", can mean different if you voice it differently. It can either sound like an order or a request. You don't sometimes notice the way you speak and when you find someone upset on you for no reason you are not able to identify the underlying cause. And that's why watching the way you speak is definitely something you should monitor.

We have the power to destroy something and at the same time mend something with the way we convey our words in our speech and the tone in our voice. A calm tone can be understood universally, and believe me even criticism will be taken right when the tone of your voice is moderate and well managed.

Today practice the tone in your voice and see the remarkable difference it has on others.

23. Kids are good observers and passive learners

If you think it's easy to take away candy from a child, then you should try doing it. No one can win an argument with children, because when they decide they decide. On the other hand, these are little pockets of happiness that have the capability of brightening up your day...

They are clean slates on which parents can write the way they want, and carve them to better individuals. But, everything comes with a disclaimer or a *conditions apply* tag because they also bear a brain, which thinks and observes at a lightning-fast speed. They of course are great learners when you teach them, but they are better off when they learn on their own.

Now you'd think, how would a child learn on its own? Well, you know they are good observers and listeners. More than what you think you know, they are watching you all the time. What you speak, you do, the way you behave, your dressing sense, the voice, expression in your eyes, absolutely anything and everything. Sometimes parents wonder, "Where did my child pick up this word from", you don't even recollect mentioning that word. Well, in that case, you need to go back to the conversation your folks in the house are having among themselves.

A child is very much capable of picking up an intention behind little gestures; if you are making an excuse with your child or making up a story, your child will pick up the actual intent behind it. Here is where they will learn how to lie. If you think the child doesn't notice, you are wrong. Also, it is more important to reason them out genuinely every time they ask you a question.

Most of the time during the growing years, parents ignore a lot of taboo questions that a child asks. They conveniently let them pass, and that's when children self-research. This is an incorrect way of learning and may mislead most of the time.

When you are open to a child, the child will open up to you. If you share a lot with them, they will be comfortable sharing their concerns, their secrets, and their reservations with you easily. After all, you are their first-ever friend and mentor.

Sometimes, when there are heated arguments in the house, have you ever wondered what goes through the child's mind. You have absolutely no idea, how a child conceives that situation and interprets it in his own way. They may not vocalize but somewhere deep within this gets registered and you may not even know the repercussion it will have in the future.

Take uttermost care about your surroundings, and what is being spoken at home and around the child. Because this is going to add as a fertilizer to the child's growing years. Childhood has to be a beautiful journey, build the base so strong that when they grow they are ready to fly heights, with values which brush pass others as well.

24. How much is too much STRESS

Everyone has a pain threshold similarly, everyone has a unique way of managing their stress. Stress in today's time is very common but what matters is how you tackle it and go by your routine.

Life is all about up's and down's, the fact is, you wouldn't value the good times if you don't experience the bad ones. If you look closely through your growth, most of your learnings would have happened in times when you were at your lowest. Good times give a boost, but it's only the lows that define your strength and teach the best lessons for life.

However, when things are not going as planned, you tend to get so overwhelmed with everything that negativity hits you. Your thought process shifts more towards the problems and that's when you start to think why it's only you who are falling prey to these situations. Somewhere you start blaming yourself and everything around you.

Most of the time the situation is not as bad as you think it is, but the way you look at it matters. This is when you consult a close one because only a neutral point of view can give you fair advice or a simple solution to your problem. An unbiased perspective will always give a favorable solution.

When you keep everything to yourself and do not vocalize, that's when it starts affecting your health mentally and physically. Stress affects your mind and body in the long term. Chronic diseases are lifestyle based and therefore attract you much easily if you are vulnerable.

A healthy mind gives you a healthy body and heart, say most of the healthcare professionals and it is true to the core. However, you need to learn to manage yourself well.

Everyone has their share of pressing situations, but if you learn to handle them effectively you will learn to distract your mind from the problem and rather focus on the solution.

Few ways to manage Stress

1. Have a calm mind and find out if there is a solution to the situation. If you cannot find a solution, discuss your problem with friends and family for an advice.

2. Meditate, this is an excellent way to relax and start off a fresh.

3. Most of the times you tend to linger around the problem too much for other things to start getting affected. Write your problem down and check if your current intensity of reaction and focus is required to the problem, if not; move on. Focus on what can be done than what cannot be done.

4. Keep a close watch on what is important and what can wait. Make a to-do list and focus on one thing at a time.

5. Discover your stress buster, start following your hobby. If you ever find yourself stressed; get back to your painting, sketching, listening to music and so on. You will instantly feel better and will be able to re align to your normal self.

6. Be aware of your thoughts, just being aware will make you get your attention back to the important tasks.

Everything can be managed in the purview of your capability. But, if you think the situation is going out of hand, only then seek professional help. Otherwise, you are just fine.

If you know when and how your mind gets affected, then you also know how to heal it. Be a self-healer.

25. Me in a nutshell... This could be you!

I know when my mind tells me there's no one like me and that the potential I have is immense. Maybe somewhere I am too hesitant to attempt and take a leap to fly. Not all of my decisions may have been right but I certainly own them in a way that I can laugh on my faults, and make necessary corrections and ensure they're not recurrent.

When I look out, I see people, people who are different and similar to me at the same time. I take time to understand them, maybe agree to disagree with some, and just choose to ignore some because somewhere, I cannot relate to them. But I like those kinds, who, despite not being similar make a lot of sense, and sometimes I do change my perspective to see things through their lenses and that's where the change takes place. I am growing, I am learning, and have come a long way to where I was.

I just wish sometimes, I could go back to where I was when I wished I should be where I am today. Not to change anything, but just to re-live my best moments with some amazing people whom I encountered in my journey, who today are somewhere else.

I always lived by the statement "My life my rules", because it always has been so encouraging for me just to be independent. Going with the flow is my way to live but at the same time, being aware of where I want to be has been in mind. Time and again I evaluate and analyse myself to check how far I have come and how much I need to walk further. Happy is always the way to go. For me, it's all about the journey; the destination arrives in no time if I am immersed in enjoying the process.

Yes, I agree to have encountered low moments because I am no different, but I have learned to enjoy the lows because I am certain of bouncing back to my highs in no time. These low times have taught me the best of lessons, which I still refer to until today. I am thankful to people who have been around during those times to support me as much as I am thankful for the situations that brought those times to me.

These were the best teachers.

I like this quote from "the fault in our stars" which I tweaked a bit ;) here goes...

You don't get to choose if you get hurt in this world...but you do have some say in who hurts you and how you react to situations, and I like my choices.

So no regrets only gratitude and smiles to everything that has been experienced so far; and very excited to all that is in store for me ahead.

Cheers to #happylife

26. Fear of Rejection

Life makes you face instances of rejection, not because it doesn't like you. On the contrary, it knows that you deserve something better, that's the way of life telling you to work harder.

This is one of the fears you may have, and that's the fear of **"Rejection".** Though it sounds like a very strong word, it's an emotion I feel, and it is the way you react to this fear of yours.

One may face rejection, by an opportunity, person, situation, or so on, and so forth. No one can escape the ups and downs that happen because, so is life, it happens to you. Therefore, your reactions and responses to these unforeseen situations matter.

Firstly and most importantly it requires acceptance from you that you are affected by rejection. Acceptance is the first step towards correction and taking charge of the situation. Most of you deny the fact that you are feeling bad and may act as if it barely matters to you. And hence unknowingly you may spend more time analyzing the situation.

Second of all, figure out the reason for being rejected. Once you find out the reason, you can work on improvising yourself. Your improved self will improve the situation around you. This makes you more prepared to overcome similar situations in the future. Also, you can help others who may go through the same. In short, your experiences make you an expert.

Thirdly, brush off the "so called" **BAD** feeling and carry the learning with you to implement henceforth. It is very important, that you do not allow the person or the rejection to affect you in the long run. If you are more concerned about "how can you be in this situation" than focusing on the actual solution, you should be alarmed because that's when it's your ego taking over.

Yes, you heard it right! Ego sometimes rises above everything else and stops you from growing and learning. Most of them would say, I don't have an ego, *why would feeling bad about my rejection relate to my ego.*

Now here is why: You always have your perspective on everything and that's why you see everything under the microscope of your analysis. But when you put yourself in the other person's shoes, only then would you have a different perspective to compare. And that is exactly when you will be able to weigh the situation on equal parameters and make the right decision on what needs to be rectified.

You need to understand that success is valued more only because of failure, similarly, you appreciate the good in people in your life only when you face some bad instances. That's how it is supposed to be. If everything was luscious green around, no one would learn how to convert an uncultivable land into a beautiful farm.

An arrow can be shot only by pulling it backward. So remember the more you are pulled back by situations, the massive would be your launch.

Rejections are your stepping stones to success.

27. My definition of Independent Self-

Well, this thought of being independent is so encouraging. However, this may sometimes make you very self-centered, depending on the extent of your choices and the decisions you make. Because; you have to deal with people all your life and it cannot be a one-way path. Of course, independence is beautiful and gives you the freedom to be the way you are and do what you want to do.

But, you should not forget that there are people who look upon you for support, people who are your responsibility, people who may not agree sometimes with your perceptions, and that's when you need to introspect yourself to see where possibly you can make changes to make certain synergies work.

A lot of people have misinterpreted the idea of having their own rules. Some take it slightly over the top by being too staunch in terms of their beliefs and likes, so much so they wouldn't budge or make even the tiniest shift in their thought process.

When you lay your own rules for yourself that are people friendly, it changes the course of the outcome in and around you. It's beautiful to be a person who is inspiring and has a positive energy which is highly contagious. A person, whose presence can brighten up a room and encourage people around to be the best version of themselves. In short, someone who is rooted and yet liberal; open to the newer perspective of life.

There is so much negativity around at the present, one needs to be risen to their own consciousness to be aware of what is happening around.

One's independence can be more directed towards not giving in to the so-called society absurd norms, breaking the boundaries of a caged potential, and making the most of the untapped self. It's more to do with spreading the light to others rather than being focused on self.

Only when self-love makes an upgrade to loving everyone genuinely and creating that connection with people around you, that's when a liberal mind can do wonders.

Today people are afraid to step into the new because of the regulations that exist. Also, one needs to function within the limits of the society and legal boundaries. But at the same time, when you see everything around, somewhere, it has been initiated by someone who wanted to grow from the old to the new and that's how the world has progressed.

Let's not be afraid to put our thoughts and make necessary changes to give an upgrade to the obsolete.

28. Why Not Learn to Talk Sense

You often get impressed with the brilliant communication skills of people. You may come across people who always according to you talk so much sense, and you are just amazed by the way they think. Have you ever wondered where these skills come from?

Everyone is constantly exposed to so much information around; and social media does the rest of the knowledge grooming. It's baffling to focus on what is worth consuming and learning but at the same time you are supposed to be aware of what needs to be skipped.

Well, it requires a continuous effort of information consumption to decide what needs to be a part of your learning and what does not. Most of your knowledge does come from the experience and the people you communicate with daily. You are constantly growing and learning; knowingly and unknowingly. What you don't know is that you are also picking up the habits of people around you.

Have you ever encountered yourself speaking a particular word or slang just because your friend or colleague or one of your relatives does so? Exactly! That's a habit you pick up unknowingly when you are in constant communication. Your style of talking along with the content that is spoken is a combination of your learning from your formal and informal knowledge and training. The formal knowledge comes from the books and academics; the informal knowledge comes from everything else that you happen to get your eyes or ears on.

You need to be aware of the way you want yourself to be groomed. Of course, there are bad influencers and spoilers around. It's only up to you what you really want to imbibe in yourself. It's very easy to be swayed into the so-called fascinating bad habits that one is exposed to, which if not managed well, can start controlling you.

You are either a prisoner of your thoughts or you can fly heights with them, the choice is yours.

You need to be in constant service to managing your mind and the rest of yourself will manage you. I cannot even emphasize how important it is to think clearly. The clearer you are the clearer will be your opinions and the instant will be your favorable responses.

On a funnier note, **Light travels faster than sound and that's why some people appear brighter before they speak ;)** *(read somewhere)*

Make yourself a better communicator with appropriate knowledge; because knowledge needs a word of mouth and that's always a better and faster way of broadcasting positivity, skills, and wisdom.

29. Being True To Self And Others Too

All of us have expectations from ourselves, however, we have more expectations from our surroundings. You often live in a bubble of high expectations from everyone around you, and when it doesn't match your satisfactory level you get upset on yourself for expecting too much.

Why can't you keep the expectations low key, this way you don't end up punishing yourself.

From a larger perspective, it's important for each of you to be true to yourself and others in terms of your relationship with everyone: Your friends, family, relatives, and acquaintances. The way you speak, behave, and share with them will define the depth of your relationship with them. Both the parties here need to be very clear of what needs to be expected and what cannot.

Most of them have a habit of being overly protective, overly expressive, or sometimes faking gestures which they otherwise wouldn't have attempted to show. This is what builds up the expectation, which is misleading and may tend to build up over a period of time.

Sometimes just to be someone's good books, people fake the rapport and that's where they don't know where to stop. One thing will always lead to another and before you know it may have gone further enough to not be able to work things backward.

Being true to others doesn't require you to be mean or rude to them, but rather just limit your conversation to where you want it to be. It will not take much effort to be the way you are; and this is definitely better than pretending to be who you are not.

The best way to go about it is to keep it simple and always speak your mind and heart without any filters, this way you will not have to go overboard and at the same time avoid someone intrude in your life as well.

It's only the expectations which lead to complications in any relationship, if only we knew how to manage people's expectations, life would be easy.

Yes, people are different, people are complex but if each learns to be true, it would make a lot of difference.

30. Looking for Perfect Imperfections-

Everyone today is searching for perfection. A perfect time to do something better, a perfect situation to feel better, a perfect life, etc etc etc,. How you really wished everything in and around you was perfect. But, nothing is perfect really in fact, nothing has to be…

Instead of looking out let's first look within. You are made unique not perfect and so are your surroundings. That's exactly why both you and everything around you fit in perfectly well. Everyone around you is your perfect match, be it your friends, family, your close ones they all exactly fit your life to make it perfect. If it was only you who made a difference you wouldn't need anyone around you. But the fact of the matter is you are because everything else is in existence and so is nature.

You get so busy judging the surroundings that you forget to compliment the beauty in it.

Let's say you are searching for a perfect career or a perfect organization. There's no such perfect career, it's only you who make it look perfect by the choices that you make to focus on. If you focus on the positive side of your professional journey, you will find it more encouraging to move ahead. If you are focused only on what is not working, it will actually not work for you.

You are constantly driving your awareness to everything around you and therefore you need to be careful of what is catching your attention.

Now let's take an example of people. People are complex, they are different you cannot tag individuals as this is a perfect person to be with or this isn't; because no one is. If you search for a perfect natured person or a person with your set of unique requirements you may not get along with anyone. There isn't any "your type" of a person with your set of likes and dislikes. You at all times would need to get accustomed to the individual as is.

The bottom line is people will be imperfect but, they will perfectly fit your life as a jigsaw puzzle. Every part of this jigsaw is scattered, you will slowly move towards each piece that fits your life perfectly at the right time of course.

And last but the most important is you, trust that you are differently built and there is no one like you. If you understand how ridiculously and insanely cool that is, you will value yourself more.

Learn to carry your imperfections as graciously and confidently as your perfections, because you are a masterpiece and only you can value or devalue yourself. No one else can, and I repeat, absolutely No One Else.

Always look for a perfect fit into an imperfect life. Everyone and everything around you are made to complement each other.

31. Introverts are extroverts who don't express

If you think introverts don't have any opinions you are absolutely wrong. Introverts are silent observers; they have all the information processed within themselves. Sometimes they are the ones who have loads to express but fail to speak or act their mind.

They may not always be fearful of expressing themselves; some may just be lazy. They are very intelligent and intense people with few words, who weigh their words when they speak. And, trust me these have more value. If you know an introvert and you are close enough to any such person you may realize that they think really deep.

Introverts behave like extroverts around the right people; is what I read somewhere, and which is absolutely true.

When they confide in you they are really true to you, because they are obviously making an effort to express it to you which is totally in contrast to what they would do otherwise.

Some of them may come across as self-centered and rude as they prefer to be secluded and stay away from socializing.

If you are an introvert, understand that sometimes you need to express because everyone always will not comprehend what you mean without you making an effort to express. Not saying that your entire nature requires a brush through, but you can definitely tweak few changes just so you are understandable.

A lot of times you may miss having the best of conversations but just because you refrain from expressing, you may loose on to bonding with great people. Letting go from time to time will expose you to your better version, you never know you may surprisingly like that change.

Some take the nature of an introvert as a sign of disinterest and keep away from creating a bond. Not everyone understands and is acceptable to the fact that they require a push to communicate and to continue a conversation or a connection.

However, they are a lot more than you think they are; and, a lot more than they speak. They definitely have a lot to express, their one liners are 'lit' and they are a gem of people when you understand them and make an effort to know them closely.

Of course, we like you the way you are and we appreciate having crisp conversations with you. Though some days, it would be a great treat to hear you express.

32. Mistakes Are Good

They say "Creativity is allowing yourself to make mistakes, but the art is which ones to keep". A lot of us fear making mistakes for a simple reason of not being able to handle the outcome of it. What one doesn't realize is that mistakes are good they teach and expose you to the ways you can handle a particular situation. In short, mistakes contribute to your self-development.

And, if you notice, this is exactly why you consult your elders whenever you are in a dilemma or between two thoughts to choose from in a situation. You obviously know that they might have been through a similar situation and would have handled it in a particular way and therefore reaching out to them is the best option to have.

The problem does not lie in going through a situation that may have been a result of a wrong decision but, the problem is not being able to look for a solution. You always need to be solution-driven. Every question has an answer and every problem has a solution. The only difference between yours and someone else's similar problem is that someone else may have a different solution than yours. It's again a perspective.

Every situation is unique to a person and therefore sometimes no similar solution may work; what you need to do is just take the next best step or necessary corrective measure and go ahead. What matters is, moving on and dealing with situations as they are. Taking time and overthinking with the problem at hand may only baffle you more.

Always remember to learn from your mistakes and carry these learnings throughout for further reference. Ensure that such a situation is not repeated in the future, because that's how one grows.

Dealing with wrong decisions in a proper frame of mind is highly important. Understand that there will always be a right and a wrong, that doesn't mean you need to always be right. In the process of correcting the wrong, you will gain experience and that's amazing about making mistakes.

Embrace your scars more than your achievements, because these scars are beautiful lessons that life teaches you.

Enjoy your journey, because one day you will tell your story on how you managed to overcome everything that today made you who you are, and maybe just maybe; someone else may get their learning from it.

33. Simple is Difficult

Have you ever noticed how complicated you can be? How many times you may have tweaked your answers to suit others. You are the best person to know yourself and no one absolutely no one knows you better than you do. Maybe there are people in your life who may be able to read you as much, but you are smarter to camouflage yourself enough to mislead others as well.

It is important to convey your heart out, though it may not be as simple as it may sound. But, somewhere you yourself need to discover what you are and, be able to express the same.

The way you treat others is the way you are actually teaching them how to treat you. The outer world is a definite mirror image of you; therefore you see the world as you are not as it is.

Sometimes, two people looking in the same direction may articulate differently simply because they are two different individuals with different outlook; carrying different experiences and substance.

Today, everything around you is so complicated, that the only control you have is over yourself, and hence you need to come across as simple as you can be so others can understand you well.

Often people try to use words and phrases which require reading between the lines. What happens here is by the time the person tries to figure out what was conveyed, he will lose you in the consequent sentences. Sometimes, the actual meaning of the dialogue may also go unnoticed. This way of communication is not only weird but also unfair to the person at the receivers' end.

Even technology has a complicated back-end but despite that, it has a simple User Interface. The developer understands the importance of simple and that an intricate UI will not do justice to the end-user.

Similarly, humans are complex, we are built that way. But nothing stops us from being simplified. Simple is indeed beautiful and has a deeper aspect.

34.   This Pandemic Has Been A Silent And Harsh Teacher

Life sometimes has distinct and weird ways of teaching you lessons which will leave a mark on you for the rest of your life. All of us are so consumed in the routine that none of us barely give this a thought, "what if something comes your way and changes your routine to a 360 degree".

Of course, there have been small and medium changes that you have adapted to, but no one wishes for such drastic changes because such changes are scary for everyone just because of your loyal love-relation with the comfort zone.

No matter how much you hear when the most successful people talk about change and adapting to the new, everyone is just listening only because of a temporary high that they get by listening to the so-called positive energy provoking talks. The effort is the second and the most important step that will lead you to that scenario of change, which has the potential to give you and your life a classy upgrade.

I, therefore, would like to throw some light on this current situation which has made people adapt to certain new normal forcefully. Though everyone has slowly worked themselves towards this normal, most of them are still complaining and waiting for everything to go back to the previous normal.

The fact of the matter is you are so accustomed to looking at the negative side of everything, that you are blinded to even peep into the positive side of it.

Here are a few things that I learned:

· Life is fragile, and expecting that everything will be the way it is today is a wishful thought. So make the most of now, because in the wait of tomorrow or the next best time; "your now" will go unattended

· State of mind is very important in every situation. The way you react and respond to every situation tells you about your state of mind. Be aware of how you react, if you think you need improvement; do not take time to take corrective action

· Your close ones require your attention. You get so busy in your daily routine that family is just taken for granted. They are the ones who require your primary attention. Make time for them regardless of your busy schedule. You need to know what is going on in their mind because more than you they may be affected by the changed situation

· Take care of yourself. Only if you are up to the mark, will you be able to take care of others. In short, practice what you preach. Ensure that the advice that you give others is first followed by you

· Be a responsible citizen, follow all the rules and guidelines that come from the authorities. It all starts from you, only if you follow the guidelines will you be able to help others and yourself to cope with the situation.

· Talk to people. Everybody is fighting their own battle, you have no idea what the other person is suffering from. If you come across someone who needs an ear, go ahead and help in your best capacity.

It is important to realize the depth of the situation and not take it lightly. At the same time, it is also important to not be boggled by the new normal, because if you give it a close thought, somewhere, certain things in your life have become easier this way. Look closely...

And also remember, no person or situation is perfect. Everything has it's own pros and cons, learn to focus on the positives, and see the changes that happen in and around you.

35.   Undervaluing one self

The primary and the most important question you need to ask yourself is: "How much do you believe in yourself?" Do you know yourself better or do you value yourself enough is what needs your attention. Have you really thought about it yet?

No one really dives deep into oneself to find out what do you want to do in life, what are your beliefs, what are your dislikes, what are your capabilities, are you challenging yourself every day, do you even vocalize what you feel for anyone without having filters at the back of your mind; fearing the judgement that you may get from others.

Everyone has immense potential to achieve what they desire, and at the same time, everyone is also very adaptable to the surroundings and situations. But what one does is, instead of acting on what is required to change the situation; everyone is waiting for the situation to change to be acted upon. This is mostly because people like to get into their routine which eventually becomes their respective comfort zone. What one doesn't realise is that they may be wasting their potential by not utilizing it up to the optimum level.

I need to urge everyone reading this to find and keep tapping your unlimited potential. This is because in various instances you often may get caught in the thought of "I do not belong here" OR "The people around me are too overwhelming for me to fit in" OR "This is not my cup of tea". Most of the time, it's you who are constantly judging your capabilities.

What you don't realize is that there is nothing that one cannot achieve. Only if one decides to "Give it a shot", the sky is the limit.

Limitations are always drawn in your head and then in your actions. If you don't have any mental limitations, and give whatever it takes to action it, there is no limit to what you can achieve.

The same human brain has built complex space crafts and completed missions beyond imagination and the same brain today maybe somewhere sitting and thinking that finding a relevant skilled job is such a difficult task to do. It's only about how you train yourself to think.

If a child's mind is trained right this habit of self-confidence and limitless potential in oneself will be achieved very early in life. Everything is a result of training, today everything that you do right from brushing your teeth to cracking bigger deals professionally is a result of training. Some are trained by others and some get trained with experiences.

Be a constant student and keep upgrading yourself. But also do not forget to value yourself, because only if you value yourself the rest of the world will. It always starts with you.

"We all make choices, but in the end, our choices make us…" (a quote I read somewhere)

36. What Women Really Want

Ahem Ahem! For some, this topic is very intriguing because it's the topic of a lifetime. Well, maybe not entirely but I will definitely try to unveil certain aspects of the topic.

Men think women are the most complex species; women think about men in the same way. Don't be surprised! It's True. How I wish both of these people knew each was thinking on similar lines, the world would have been more easy-going.

Well firstly, there have been a lot of changes in the way everything functions today. If I talk about ancient times, most of the women were looked down upon and did not have the privilege of representing themselves independently. Yet today, there are social norms that are still made considering they are less important than their significant other.

However, women of today know what they want, what they like, and what they want to do in life. They want to be the thinkers and the doers of the society, as capable as they are; they want their space and their word to be counted. Not because it requires to be counted, but because it is certainly worth giving serious thought.

Today, as a daughter she wants to be her father's support and mother's best friend; as a sister, she wants to be discussing the household responsibilities with her siblings; as a partner, she wants to hold hands and walk shoulder to shoulder at every stage of their life.

As a child, a girl needs to be treated equally and respectfully. She needs an equal opportunity to prove herself and be successful. She needs to be heard clearly and be understood as to why she has such opinions that differ.

She is emotional but that is definitely not a sign of weakness, on the contrary, that's her strength of not shying away from showing her tears. She doesn't want to be judged at all stages of life specifically on her character when she represents herself boldly and takes certain decisions. Her relationship status is often questioned if she moves from one relationship to another, just because the previous one didn't work for some reason.

She is her own strength and she knows that, she doesn't require any external source to put her broken pieces back in place. However, she doesn't mind someone who takes the responsibility of taking care of her and regales her.

She not only wants to make her point but at the same time, gracefully accepts that there might be another point of view. And, therefore doesn't mind compromising on someone else's decision despite sometimes not agreeing with it fully, which is just because she truly cares.

Yes, there may be differences because all days are not the same. She does get mad but this is purely superficial, the sooner you understand, the better you'd be able to manage her.

If you set her free she is the best thing that will happen to you, but if you try to cage her she will make it really miserable for you, I couldn't have put it more subtly.

Enjoy her company and you will know how amazing these beautiful creations are. For only women, are given the privilege of giving life to another being.

37. Do We Understand Men Yet?-

Everyone is focusing mainly on how complex women are and we leave these guys on their own. They definitely deserve to be heard and to be understood at the same time. We have always at some point in time voiced this phrase "Men will be Men". Yes, they are one of their kind. One doesn't really take an effort to know them deeply because most of the time, they themselves don't vocalize.

They go with the "it's okay" thought which refrains them to speak and express what they genuinely feel. And most of the time just to avoid conflict they may just agree to what you want.

They are flamboyant in nature and that's how they behave with their pals, most of the men behave their real selves only with their friends. Their immediate family would not even know that side of them exists. They are at their best when they are with friends. Observant to the core, they may pick things that you may not realize are noticeable in you.

In their growing up years, they are constantly looking for that perfect environment. Very rarely a brother to brother or a brother to sister will share their heart and mind. Even if they do, they will share only 40% of their thoughts. They don't trust anyone entirely very easily or maybe they're too lazy to do so either.

"Girls" happens to be their favorite topic among friends. But there is a stark difference in how they describe their kind of girl to their friends and how they want her to be in real. You will be totally shocked if you actually get to know their inside story.

Their minds are creative and their focus is unwavering when it comes to their career, only a few may not be that career-driven either due to their lethargic nature or maybe because they are still figuring it out. Otherwise, guys do always strive to know their subject.

Men seem to have no emotions because they are not the ones who emote that easily, but that doesn't mean that they are insensitive. They definitely get affected but they choose not to emote in public. Some men do express with close ones but that too in extreme situations. They just share their heart with their inner circle which may not necessarily be their family.

We sometimes think men wouldn't ever need to be heard but on the contrary, they crave to be heard. Once they find that someone who they trust and who is all ears, they will pour their heart out. They definitely want to be taken care of, they are constantly searching for this quality in a partner, if they happen to find one such bond they are set to give it all to the relation.

As much as they look stronger than the women, they are weaker emotionally and need that shoulder to just be there.

A man will always want his women stronger than him, but he will not vocalize for the simple reason of not letting her know that he needs her more than she does.

38. Our Figurative Journeys-

Life is a Journey" this sounds like a complex cliché. But is it really?! This question needs to be felt, not to be asked. The best part of life is, everyone has a unique story but, not everyone is a good storyteller.

If you look closely everything around you has happened for a reason, the smallest thing that has changed in your life has made a significant impact which has brought you to where you are today. However, we often take things very lightly, some of them at least.

Almost all of you'll have had certain small instances in life which brought about a lot of change. Maybe shifting to a new place made you encounter new opportunities, bumping into a stranger in your office, school, or someplace else, has made you the best of friends. Or maybe, meeting with an accident has changed you completely and made you look at life differently.

How many of you'll take a moment to realize where they are and what have they been through so far. Have you ever noticed the changes you have been making unknowingly or the changes some of the situations have compelled you to make in your life? You often are exposed to change unknowingly.

Change is constant and it's only change that leads to growth.

How I wish life's journey was as good as planning a holiday, just a couple of logistics to be taken care of and we are good to go. Life is unpredictable and, that's what makes the journey complex and interesting. Before you think you know all the answers to life, it changes the question; you are left perplexed as to what just happened

Life requires to be seen through a birds-eye view and then to be consumed and understood bit by bit. Like every tiny little drop of water is responsible to create a vast deep ocean. Small steps that you take, make bigger differences in your life.

Always look around for inspiration and look within for answers. Only you know what you want and most of you aren't very clear on that yet.

A journey is better lived and enjoyed when we are sure of where we are heading and that's a much bigger question when it comes to where you want to go and what you want to be.

Of course, everything may not go as planned, but during the course of your journey, you are always free to make changes that are good then.

Make sure you have good company in your journey, cuz no journey is complete without beautiful people around you. And these are the ones which make our lives worth living. Life is too valuable to be boggled with people and thoughts which affect you and slow you down. Learn to give away and let go of whatever seems heavy on your heart and mind. It's totally not worth it.

Learn to accept and move on from everything that no longer serves the benefit to your peace of mind. Everything worth giving your attention and heart will always find a way

out in your life. Otherwise, there is always a newer aspect ahead in store.

39. No Tree Has Ever Grown Under A Banyan Tree-

Nature has always been a very resourceful teacher. There is an old Indian saying that nothing ever grows below a banyan tree. And this is precisely how life happens to all of us, but we seldom realize that this way is the best way it can be done.

Birds take care of their li'l ones until they are on their own and then leave them to build their lives. Mother giraffes kick their newborn immediately after it is born. The baby shivers with weak limbs, the mother still does this act a couple of times until the baby trembles and shakes but finally stands on her own feet. This is quite an earth-shaking event. But, the giraffe does this just to make the baby ready for her self defence against the wild animals who are always looking for their easy prey.

Similarly, a banyan tree ensures it provides shelter and comfort. Though it grows huge enough expanding its branches nothing grows beneath the tree. Such are most of the leaders, they will support you, comfort you, and give you whatever you need for your growth but when it is time for you to step up, they will want you to be on your own. This act is taken as rude behavior by most people but when they actually understand the crux of this gesture, they realize that this is the best way a person can learn. Nobody really learns by leaning on anyone's shoulders.

Remember, right from your kinder garden days no matter how much your parents and your teachers taught you the alphabets and the numbers; at the end of the day, it is you who had to write your exam paper. Therefore, no matter how much support you have through your life, certain things need only you to be in the spotlight and that time no one but only you will be responsible for the outcome.

This is probably the best way to teach. Independence makes you realize your potential, without it you would always doubt to take the next step on your own. At some point, the parent has to let go of the child's hand while teaching him to walk. As much as it is exciting for the child to experience the walk independently, the parent is more than excited.

So whenever you feel that your parent, your teacher, your guide or your mentor is not supporting you for some work and wants you to do things and take ownership and responsibility. Trust me! They are not being rude or less concerned about you. On the contrary, they want you to see what they are seeing and that's your true potential and your growth.

40. Sometimes, Even Love Needs Validation

Certain relations may be more than what they appear to you. And, some of you don't even wait for a situation to make you get the existential aspect of a relation. You are in so much rush to name everything that when you want to be in love you hold on to the next good conversation you have, the next slightly good person you meet, or the next amazing thought of a person you get.

You don't even allow yourself to look at the larger picture. Relations these days are therefore short-lived, you are in so much hurry to start a relationship and at the same time in a rush to end something good. This is what makes everything very superficial.

Before either of you tap the depth of a relationship you are out of it already.

People are different, people are unique and at the same time, they will somewhere or the other fit your likeable or not so likeable criteria.

That doesn't mean if someone is very close to your choices of likes and dislikes, you conclude that this is the one! If this was the case we could have had relationships with a quarter of the World.

Relationships are fragile. If the base is not built strongly the longevity may get affected.

So when is that you consider something to be going where you actually want it to:

- Trust the vibe, your vibe will never fail you. If you think you have a great vibe that can be considered as the first validation that you get along well.

- Communication is very important. If you can communicate with the person genuinely without any filters then that's one of the great signs.

- Genuineness and intent is another important aspect. If the conversation was initiated merely to "let's see if this works" you are talking to the person only to figure out if this would work. Most of the thick relations are free-flowing, they never started with a casual agenda. Anything that starts with a casual agenda, will need validation at all times.

- Maturity, is when you understand that there may not always be sugar-coated conversations but may also be slightly heated disagreements. And it is the post disagreement reactions and come-backs that define a relationship. If your ego is mightier than the person you love, it's not gonna work on a one-way compromise.

- It's sad that most of them want to get into a relationship just because they are missing being in one. These are the ones who may tend to move quickly into another just because they were too fast in taking a call that this ain't working. Because the idea is just to arrive at a conclusion too fast and not take time to work on it.

- Eventually, not every relationship is perfect. There will always be something which you may not like as a trait in a person, but that doesn't nullify the other good qualities. Searching for perfect is never an idea, because, no one is perfect and, neither are you. You just need to find "your perfect" in an imperfect person or relation.

Don't be with someone you can live with; be with someone you cannot live without.

41. My Last Chance To Work On Self

Everyone loves to procrastinate. Everything that you do is just because you either are forced or either you love to do what you do. If you get an account of how many activities that you do during the day are a part of your lifestyle only because you love to do them, you will be surprised that the weight will be more on stuff that you are required to do, not because you love to do but because it has become a necessity; and this is just primarily because you don't have an option.

How many of you would right now quit your respective jobs if it was not required for you to get food on the table? How many of you would have wanted to change the people around you? How many would want to escape from their respective routines? How everyone wishes life was one fairy tale where everything was beautiful, out of this world, and larger than life. The life, the food, the parties, the friends, the close ones, so on and so forth, how we wish we had our choices on these...

But, you need to come down to the realization that everything is not painted in bright colors that you so wished. However, it is upon you how you want to make your life worth living.

Most of you live each day thinking that things will change, but only a few take the onus to change things within you to change things around you. This is your chance to work on yourself. The question is, when are you going to implement changes in you? When? How much time do you want to spend concentrating on what is going wrong instead of what has gone right to-date and what can further make a difference?

The fact of the matter is, no one is going to take that decision for you. It's only you who will have to take that call for yourself. Stop playing victim to your comfort zone, nothing extraordinary has ever happened in the so-called "cushioned space" of your comfort zone. You have to take bigger and different decisions sometimes to breakthrough and to re-discover yourself along with your potential.

If I take my life as an example: I certainly have experienced difficulty in moving into the new, in taking up something independently. My biggest fear was after my first stint in a healthcare setup when I'd got an opportunity to prove my individual potential without my mentor who supported guided me in my previous organization. I remember how much shivers I'd had before taking up that opportunity and saying "yes" to it. However, I was surprised at how much I could deliver and was amazed at what results I could bring. From then on, I started my journey of exploring my potential through every new challenge.

Today here I am, though I still have a long way to go, so far so good!

In the midst of postponing every move, you often waste time and find reasons that stop you from doing things that may just change the course of your lives. However, just step back and think why would you want to change that or take it up. You may just find your answer.

Think about it, ***WHAT IF THIS WAS YOUR LAST CHANCE TO WORK ON YOURSELF***, would you still give up on you.

If you can't change things around you, change things within you, the time is NOW or NEVER, because; just to remind you the clock is doing its job diligently.

42. Some Mindless Ramblings got interesting

Capability

The blue blanket which is covering us is not only capable of protecting us but also has a potential to destroy every being. Never do we question everything around us. As a kid, I had too many questions.

Unrevealed

Strangely, we exist with these so-called technologies today, but at the same time, some basic truths may still have not revealed themselves. I do know someday, it's gonna be a huge surprise for all of us.

Time

A part of me always wanted to grow fast to know what all is in store for me, but everyone has to go through the 365-day cycle to grow a year older. Now, I wish that the cycle could move a bit slow because so much needs to be done.

Belief

Magic happens when you believe, this is something I learned and it's so profoundly amazing. Nothing ever happens within you and becomes a part of your life without you truly believing. One such reality is you will always depend on an external factor when in dire situation. Whom do you call out for help in your heart when you see absolutely no escape from a situation? Is it God? Is it the Universe? Or is it an energy that you believe? When you are out of that situation, somewhere you do believe that you were helped by that source in some way or the other. Strange but true!

Unknown

Do you know we all have a right to choose our parents, before being born to them? I do not want to dive too deep into this one! But I just like the idea of being able to do that. I feel this was the best decision I ever made.

Expectations

He who wants her to be the best suited for self doesn't realize that she also wants the same in him. But in the process of wanting the best in her, he fails to make himself the best fit.

Existence

We all exist because we coexist with people and nature however, somewhere I feel we are missing harmony. And, in the run of finding our own identity, we forget the importance of our surroundings. Have we ever wondered suddenly why are natural calamities so common? The world is struggling to heal itself and in the struggle, we are the ones who have become the victims of its change. Let's practice the new normal, I am not sure how much of it will get back to the previous normal.

Positivity is what the world needs for now, an attitude of gratitude can go a long way.

43. In The Pool Of Thoughts, Learn To FOCUS

At any given point our mind is constantly at work. It has millions of thoughts running without any control over what needs to be thought and what is unimportant. Distraction is a place that doesn't allow you to focus on the task at hand. For the most of them, it is a very comfortable space to be and some can spend hours thinking and focusing on nothing but just random thoughts. Most of the minds run at a lightning speed where one doesn't know where to stop.

The outcome of this is seen in the speech, as one speaks mindlessly because gathering thoughts becomes difficult. People have a tendency to think multiple things at the same time and therefore find it difficult to express, even though they might be very intellectual they may not be able to convey their mind into words.

You often are so consumed in thinking that you don't want to take control of your thoughts and re-direct them. If one learns how to channelize their thoughts to a productive thought process, it would have created so much mind-space and eliminated the clutter.

Easy as it sounds it ain't. Firstly, it requires acceptance and second of all, it requires a will to change. Only once one decides that something needs to be worked on does one take a step further into changing things.

Here are a few things one can follow:

1. Being aware of your thoughts, is a primary thing one needs to do. Whenever you notice yourself caught in a trance of thoughts, bring your attention back to the current area of focus.

2. Thinkers are creative people, and everything that has come your way positive and negative has come because you have thought about it. Know the importance of time. Of course, thinking is a good exercise however one needs to know how much time to put in.

3. Do not try to multi-task. As much as everyone thinks multi-tasking is a skill, our minds are not built to multi-task. One can only give 100percent focus to one task at any given point. When one focuses on multiple tasks at the same time, the focus is divided and therefore productive outcome is not achieved in either of the tasks.

4. Meditate, this is a beautiful way of gathering your thoughts and calming yourself in the midst of the ocean of thoughts running in your mind. It definitely helps if practiced over a period of time.

5. Exercise. Now, this could just be skipping, jogging, or an early morning stroll but exercise has a significant impact on your blood circulation, it increases the heart rate which results in more oxygen pumped into the brain.

6. Stay positive. Ensure that your thoughts are always positive. Positive thoughts help you have positive energy throughout the day.

7. Speak to people who help you learn. Being in the company of people who are always encouraging, empowering, and knowledgeable help you grow. So watch your company and keep away from people who drain your energy levels with negativity.

Know that you are the master of your mind, don't be the slave. Act and channelize the right thoughts and the right energy.

44. Festivities these days are enjoyed superficially

I remember how excited I was for every festival and celebration we had. It was not about the stuff we do during those festivals, but it's the people I enjoyed with. Though I met my friends, neighbours, and extended family every second day. I was still super excited to get up and get going on the day of celebration just to meet all of them.

Today it is so much different, everybody is getting tonnes of forwards and these forwards are merely sent across just because one needs to pass on a wish and that too without any feelings or sentiments. Sometimes we forward the same message to a person twice without realizing that we already wished the person, that's how insensitive it gets.

Most of them are not dressed for the occasion, they are social media dressed. Only trying to prove on social media, how colorful and amazing their life is. However, I feel that the ones who are really enjoying, don't need a social media post. They're just so busy living the moment that most of them forget to click pictures. No, I am not saying that it is wrong to post pictures or click them during occasions; it's just that everything looks so "done up" in the pictures than in real.

People have started adding filters to their real-life as they add to their posts on social media. In reality, barely even want to convey greetings to their extended families or pay a visit to them.

Lives have become so crazily materialistic that the only ones we are close to (currently) are the office colleagues or the people you come in contact with every day. And when we move on to new jobs, schools, colleges, and homes we have a new set of people who come in contact; the old ones, at least a few are conveniently forgotten.

Have you ever wondered when you genuinely call a person just to check in on them, they still ask you the actual reason for your call and maybe wait till the end of the call till you say "I really called you just like that".This is what we are going towards, no one really believes when you genuinely care.

Of course, life happens to everybody but let's not make relations superficially. Let's connect heart to heart with people and make these bonds stronger, not because we require them, but these are the relations which can go a long way, make you a better person, and help you pause from your otherwise monotonous life.

45. Your Behaviour patterns

Do you know where does your behaviour come from? We all know that all of us have certain behavioural pattern, not all may react similarly to similar situations. Everyone has their likes and dislikes and each behaves differently.

These behaviours are majorly influenced by our surroundings and situations. A child is constantly observing the people they are exposed to, the way they speak to the child and the way people are communicating among themselves.

If we take examples here, a child who is always been spoken affectionately will only understand and speak accordingly. Even if the parents have to make the child understand they will very softly convey the child about the right and the wrong and this becomes a part of the child's behavior as well.

On the other hand, if the child is constantly yelled at and spoken to in an irritable tone, the child also becomes irritable and behaves similarly. Now, this is where the child understands the difference in the voice tone and adapts to it.

Many a time because of certain situations, certain fears are developed in all of us. Some have water phobia just because once they experienced suffocating, they decided not to enter the pool. Some may have experienced bike or car accident and stopped riding/driving from then on. These are all experiences which stay with us and change our pattern of behaviour towards certain things.

Only when one makes an effort to change something would they be able to make a conscious effort to correct certain thought processes in them. Let's say someone is short-tempered, in such cases, one must take time to compose before reacting aggressively. If one takes time to react, the response becomes favourable to the situation and then to the person it may have been directed towards.

Also, it may occur to you that sometimes the opposite person requires correction; here in this case we don't have much control over how people react. However, we certainly have control over our response, choose your response wisely and you will see a change in the opposite person.

We are often controlled by our mind, and most of the times the mind focuses on negative first. For us to focus on the positive one needs to train the mind. Practice makes everything easy; repetition is the easiest way to perfect anything.

When people are in a bad mood or stressed about something they will focus on the bad that is happening and continue to be in that mode. What one doesn't realize is that they are being consumed by the negativity and therefore everything around them appears to blur and uncertain.

One has to shift the energy deliberately and focus on the positive in every situation because it is really easy to be swayed by the negative but when you get out of the negative to find your positive in every situation; you become stronger each time.

Fix your own vibe before pointing out on someone else's negativity.

46. Trans' Different But Beautiful

Everyone is struggling with themselves and fighting their own battle. The fight sometimes is so difficult that people take years to come out and express.

One such fight is self-identity in transgender. Firstly our society is so closed to accept the fact that such struggles exist. And, more so the primary reason for the fear of acceptance for someone who is going through the struggle is just because of the outer world. It would have been so easy if the outer world was so accepting.

I have encountered a couple of people who were going through such a struggle, and have faced extreme opinions and stares from people not only from their outer circle of acquaintances but also from their inner circle, including parents. And when your own parents are not accepting you the way you are it becomes more difficult.

Some fight to get out of their own body and want to go through changes, thankfully the western world is much open and allows people to have their own stands, and are pretty accepting of the fact.

However, one doesn't realize that the topic for such individuals is so intricate and sensitive both at the same time that if it's not handled properly may hurt feelings. Though, the ones I know have come out so strongly that they have made their own way and are living gracefully in this so-called "judgemental" world.

I always feel a sense of strength in them because only they can understand their pain, and only they know, it takes a powerful person to live life against society and essentially against their own family's will.

Because of certain decisions that they want to take, most of them are forced to live separately. This makes it so much more difficult for them because of course during these times they do miss their families a lot. It would have been so much better if they could have been more acceptable to the fact that, yes; some people are differently beautiful, things would have been easier.

I think we have come a long way to be accepting the nature and everyone part of it. We are all human after all just made differently. It's time for us to accept them and their right to be able to be gracefully able to live the way they want to.

47. Forgive But Never Forget

I have always heard people saying "Forgive and Forget". But I think forgiving is more important to move on. However, most of the time it is difficult to forget, it somehow stays at the back of your mind.

We all have had good and bad instances in the past, and specifically, we all carry a few of them through our journey because somewhere they have created an impact on us.

As each drop of water is instrumental in creating an ocean, many such instances make us who we are and the way our reflexes work. Then, there are situations, people, and incidents that affect us so much and so deeply that forgetting them becomes next to impossible. Even when time goes by, even if it does not create an impact on your routine as it did previously, it certainly brings your attention to a standstill.

Of course, some instances may involve people and that's when things sometimes get sour between the two of you'll; where you only have two choices either you move on from the person or you move on from the situation. As difficult as it is to deal with the former here, the latter is no easy as well. When you move on from a situation and forgive the person the instance remains at the back of your mind, and the impact influences your behavior towards the person because you still have an impact of the situation somewhere in the subconscious.

One needs to be matured to deal with this, and only as you learn to deal with it, you become better at handling such situations. The point here is, people in your life are important, instances are temporary. Essentially, what you require to do is to decide whether or not would you be ready to lose the person. Because only you know the gravity of the situation and the importance of the person in your life.

It certainly takes a big heart to forgive but a bigger conscience to forget.

I think one should never forget an impact caused by a person or a situation, good or bad because at some point in time this helped you to grow. And more so, you became stronger and grew out of the situation. The larger perspective is to understand that we ought to forgive a lot of times not because the person or the situation deserves it, but only because you need to move on.

48. Are You Open To Correct Yourself?

We learn and we grow this is a no-brainer, however, while we are learning we are also upgrading and getting rid of our previous perspectives and understanding of certain aspects of people and situations. The previous perceptions may be obsolete and therefore one has to continuously be in the growth mode.

Most of the time it gets difficult for people to leave the older self, and that's where the growth stops. One needs to be open to be wanting to grow, and for the same one needs to learn from their own mistakes.

The thing with "MISTAKES" is that one only realizes after they are done making them. Because only the outcome will make you realize that you shouldn't have taken that path or done a particular thing in that manner.

No one ever learns from a smooth sailing life. "Experience" is what a person gets once one commits various mistakes but eventually learns a better way to handle a similar situation in the future.

Always be open to correct yourself from anybody and everybody, the ones who give you advice are only thinking good for you. Though it is also okay to self-analyse what you think is right and discuss. An argument doesn't lead you anywhere a healthy discussion always does and also leads you to a changed perspective.

Sometimes one is not open to learning from people who they don't like in the first place, because they think the intent may not be right or, for a simple reason of not wanting to listen to them. I think if the learning and if the advice is worth taking you should take it from anyone regardless of your likability; because learning, is a learning, is a learning; point-blank. If one is open to growth and has an ear, one will not have anything come in between their learning.

If you notice the most open to learning are the most successful people because they have always been in the growth mode.

Be the one who at all times is observant of everything and absorbs the surroundings with an eye which is as curious as a child. Ready to have an own perspective, ready to learn, ready to ask questions, and ready to make mistakes because the actual learning starts from the first fall before you walk.

49. Books Make You Mentally Travel To Places You Have Never Been Physically-

Often we take the power of words for granted. Words have an amazing way to change and shift a lot of thinks within.

Life is all about different experiences one goes through and learns from. And most of them when they learn from such experienced instances they get an insight into what mistakes one can avoid.

Books are one such source that we can lean on for inspiration and perspective at the same time. I am glad that these days writers are putting their thoughts so openly which exactly fits one's life and helps them understand and find a solution.

It's amazing how our lives are so interlinked and can help each other move ahead. The value that books add to our life is underrated and underestimated. Only an avid reader can understand what a non-reader is missing.

There is no difference between a literate person and an illiterate person if one is not reading. (Read somewhere)

Also if someone had a flair for writing, they need not refrain from putting their thoughts on paper cuz you never know what may just change someone's thought process. Today, everyone is so busy to even be aware of the words said and the lessons learned that they may miss on to most of the major punch lines that they might learn from. Hustling through the day is a thing these days, most of them are acting busy, very few among them are actually productive.

Authors are putting so much effort into conveying their entire life's experiences in a 5–6 hour read, most of these books are really worth a takeaway. Because someone else's past experience might be someone else's lesson that can be applied in the future.

What amazes me that, books can make you take a ride into instances which never really occurred in your life, but the way someone puts it into words compels you to live the moment.

Well, not everyone loves to read, but if you choose to start with books with interesting content, you surely will at least try to get your hands on a few of the gems.

Books serve to show a person that those original thoughts of yours are not so original at all..(read somewhere)

Reading is a beautiful joy ride, some of them I'd love to take trips with multiple times...

50. Ideas, If Not Implemented On-Time, May Get Obsolete

Everyone has had their eureka moments, where they get an idea which they thought was out of the box but soon it fizzled out without even being implemented or even thought again. However, one doesn't realize the importance of an idea, because it is definitely not like a usual thought that pops into your mind.

"My mind is like a lightning, one brilliant flash and then… it's all gone". I don't know who put it so beautifully but when I came across this line I had a hearty laugh in my head.

Because people take their thoughts casually most of the time, some of these thoughts die before they're born. If you look around you, everything around you is sitting with you today because of someone's thought, or an idea once someone had. Right from your laptop, to your house, to your education system everything was an idea once which came to perspective.

It's fun when your tiniest thought, manifests into a huge deal and then changes the lives of many around you. How I wish people are more aware of their thoughts, inventions would have been faster and we would have been exposed to so many newer concepts.

Ideas are progressive by nature the more you implement and keep going in the direction they help you improvise at all times. No success comes without failures and no right would be worth without a wrong. So let's not have fear of losing out on the time, or fear of not succeeding; because only the ones who keep going will always find a way to succeed.

One good thing about our thoughts is that you completely own them and whatever happens they're a part of you. It's wonderful when these grow to an actual physical concept.

Now, how does one know which ones to keep, well, you have to trust your gut for that. Write down your thoughts and work around them, give them a generous amount of time and attention over a period, so much so you see them grow and when you think they are ready to be worked upon, don't waste a single moment. This is how huge empires were built, the ocean got its depth, and the mountain got their height.

Success for everyone comes in their own time, and it finds its way after the exact amount of effort, because for each is its own. You will find yours in your timeline, don't compare your life to someone else's because everyone has a unique journey, and everyone has a unique story.

Make your story someone else's guideline to success...

51. 5 Signs that you like being ordinary

They say everyone is different and unique, however, I feel everyone also gets an equal opportunity to change themselves. The only difference is some choose to change, and some choose not to. The journey for everyone is precisely basis the decisions they make. The world is divided into two halves I feel; the ordinary and the extraordinary, only the 'extra' is what makes the massive difference.

5 Signs that you like being ordinary:

1. You are too adamant to change: Change is something that is inevitable, and which is the need of the hour. One can get different results only when they are ready to change and act differently. Otherwise, the growth wouldn't be as swift as you expect it to be. The key is to be aware of what you want and if you are doing your bit to get there. Everyone wants the best for them, but no one really wants to actively work for it.

2. The "it's Okay" attitude: The "It's okay" is an attitude either of the lazy or of people who think they know it all and don't really care. They make it an excuse because they do not want to get up and get going. Nothing drives them and they just get into the lethargic mode. These are the ones who just take things and accept things the way they are. They want a better life but are not willing to give what it takes and therefore hide behind their "it's okay attitude".

3. *You are too comfortable enjoying the ordinary life:* Most of you start loving the routine you are into and therefore no motivation can help you get rid of the routine. You get too comfy in enjoying the so-called mediocre life. Which can only be changed if one has a very very strong reason /a goal or a dream that would drive them off the routine.

4. *Motivation only gives a temporary high:* The information that you have is raw until you benefit from it and the only way to benefit from it is by applying that information to gain experience. Motivation is one such dose of learning that needs direction; only if directed and channelized appropriately would it be helpful for your growth and productivity. It is very easy to get back to your old self; one needs to have immense self-control and perseverance to be who you want to be.

5. *Growth is never the goal:* When a person becomes content with what one has, growth is never a goal. The only goal is to go by the day and just merely survive through. And that's where the thought process comes to a standstill.

Guidance through the journey of life comes only through your upbringing, your surroundings, and your experiences. Whereas, success comes only after relevant work is put in the direction of the goal. Take a decision of either adding that "Extra" in your life or living in the "Ordinary"... #onelife

52. It's Okay To Not be Okay

We don't have similar looking days every day. There are good days and there are not so good days. And sometimes it's totally Okay

Only because of the presence of the not so good days we value the better ones and that's precisely why the bad exists in a good, a day exists after a dark night, and everyone wades through the traffic of challenges before they achieve success.

The only thing here one needs to understand is that not all days are bright, also it's the way one handles their lows defines the attitude of the person. One needs to give attention to their lows as well, just to introspect and move on to the next better emotion and the next better focus.

Focus changes everything, if you learn to focus right you can manage yourself better.

If you observe a crying baby, everyone around the baby only tries to change the attention of the baby. The moment the baby gets distracted, it stops crying. What happens here is that the focus is changed, and the mood switch takes place. Such is the way we are built, but as we grow manipulating our mind becomes slightly difficult. However, it's definitely **not impossible** to shift focus.

Also, sometimes you may not be able to shift your thoughts to the positive because the situation may be grave or difficult. In that case, just being there at that point in time is important, not everything may require your immediate attention and action. Sometimes, it's okay to live in the moment because it is yours and only you know how you feel. Giving importance to your lows is essential as well because that's when you understand yourself better and learn to divert from that moment.

Most of the people are lucky to have someone with whom they can vent it out. On the other hand, some may not be comfortable speaking their heart out and that's completely alright. Letting your self be is also respecting your emotions and yourself. However, everyone has their secret to changing their mood; some lean on their favourite binge food, some listen to their favourite songs, some go on drives and some have a passion/art to lean on to. Whatever it is, at that point it is your only best focus or space to be in.

There are people who find it difficult to express themselves, and therefore they take humour or silence as their defence during their low times. As much as their close ones claim it's easy to understand them, only they know that no one is going to exactly understand what goes through them.

Time is an amazing teacher, give "Time", time to heal you. At the same time, don't take too much time to bounce back.

53. Don't wait for Horoscopes to tell your future... Create one..

It's a feel-good factor for a lot of people to read their horoscopes every morning to check how their day looks like. They are so excited to read it and at the same time, they blindly believe it. Though it's great psychology since you live in that positive energy it actually works for you.

I think it's a placebo effect though, which is good if it's working right, however in the long run one needs to take the charge and ownership of their own life and results. Our thoughts define us and it's our thoughts that guide us through. Where do these thoughts come from?

Well, what you think is precisely what you have believed, your journey of self-growth comprises of your learning over the period. These learnings primarily come from your upbringing and then your surrounding but along with that, every individual has self-discipline. It's the discipline that helps to form the character of an individual.

Everyone has dreams, but not everyone focuses on achieving them. If we ever sit ourselves down to ask ourselves "WHAT WE REALLY WANT?", we may get our answers. Some may take time to get there; it is a continuous effort that one needs to take to visualize themselves, implement, and work towards it bit by bit.

Even one step taken towards working on something is a step closer to achieving what you desire.

Yes, life is only finite but it's certainly not short. It is easy to dream with closed eyes, but if one really wants something, it needs to be worked on with open eyes. Dreams do come true but there are no free lunches; hard-work and perseverance are required to experience the dreams for real.

Everyone is born unique, no similar people will experience the same good stuff mentioned in the horoscope. If you are ready to create your blueprint, you will not need to keep a check on your horoscope.

The next time you want to know about your day and your future, simply be aware of what has been worked on so far.

54. SHE

She is always dazzling, but few only see her shine A minute of intelligence and the second instance of childish nature always confuses people. A lot of things that she carries inside of her are not acceptable and therefore she chooses not to disclose that side of her to the world. Her strength lies in her emotion but is always mistaken for her weakness. A master of all that she is, able to manage all the tasks as skilfully, as if she was trained well in advance and therefore, making it seem effortless.

She represents every relation with grace and conducts it with ease, understanding her for her significant other may be complicated at times ;) but yeah that's her.

Her only drawback is that she expresses very strongly which may be overwhelming sometimes. She has an ocean within her, and no one can imagine the depth of it. She can transform an apartment into a home and if she wants to, she can create hell out of it as well, you choose what you want. Treat her well, and you know you will get the best of her, the moment you brush on to her wrong side, you will get the taste of her not so easy to digest sarcasm.

She is known to be gossiping however no one would realize the pleasure of venting out, not to complain, but just so she empties her already so very preoccupied mind.

Her thoughts run faster than yours, by the time you are at your 5th move she is already on her 100th and that's already planned in her head. A skill that no man can understand is her ability to switch moods as swiftly as people change from one outfit to another.

Yes, she is a woman, she seems confused at times, she may overreact, may tell you things you don't expect her to, maybe difficult, maybe annoying, maybe weird but she has an inherent quality to nurture and therefore will create the best space for you in her life regardless of the relationship you have with her.

Help her help you complete your life.

55. We Never Really Grow Up, We Only Learn How To Act In Public

I have read this phrase somewhere, and I can't tell you how much this line made me think. We all have gone through the process of understanding what is right and what is wrong most of these learnings come from our parents.

And how much ever we try and make changes in the way we behave externally, somewhere inside, we are that same child who once liked to behave in a certain manner, sit on the sofa shabbily, watch TV while lying down and eat the favorite food so fast as if someone's gonna eat it from our plate.

How we wished we didn't require behaving like adults. If it was okay to behave the way we wanted to, trust me no one would behave the way they do today.

Have you encountered yourself refraining from reacting to something exciting or stopped yourself from laughing too hard just because you are in the midst of a formal company; of course we have. Well, not that we don't like our changed self, but we so wished there was freedom to do things which we today otherwise wouldn't.

There have been instances where people have told me not to laugh too loudly or to stop reacting extremely, or this is not supposed to be your expression in public. But that's me, I never hold myself from behaving in a certain manner and I think it's completely me, and it's okay if people think it's too much sometimes. I am comfortable with it, so are my closest folks and, that's what matters

The bottom line is everyone is required to change basis the external environment. I feel there is so much expectation out there, everyone is ought to fulfil these expectations.

If you really ask what people wish, they will just want to enjoy life, doing the set of things they like. But then reality hits right in the head and everyone has to face this real world of grown-ups and intellects.

If only LIFE was all about chilling, people would have lived differently.

But not to forget we all have a purpose here, but at the same time let's not forget to bring out the child in us once in a while.

Keep the child in you always alive and don't ever shy away from expressing.

56. The One Who Loves The Least Controls The Relationship...

Here is something I have been observing but was not really able to believe. Slowly it got me and I think this is what it boils down to.

Relations are many but the one common thing between them is love. However, both involved in a relationship may not share the same "unit" of love. I say unit here because I am not sure how love can be quantified. Unconditional is a term given when people like to exaggerate their affection towards the other but trust me no one loves you more than your parents and I mean "NO ONE".

Well, whatever I have said so far, and will be saying henceforth is purely my perspective and my opinion on a subject, of course, people can think differently.

Let's start with our relationship with parents, they give it all for us and we always would take them for granted, at some point or the other this has been realized by a lot of people but very few have gathered the sense or felt the necessity of going up to them and saying "I am sorry, I have been taking you for granted". Whatever is said and done, in the end, it is only the parents who have to be on the adjusting side, they are the ones who are pretty much saying yes to what their children want. And sometimes children find a way in convincing them, either way, parents love you unconditionally and that's about it.

Friends are the other set of people who we get close to as we move ahead in our life, and here's a sad truth; even best friends don't like each other equally. Have you ever witnessed your best friend suddenly turn into a stranger? Well... I have, and that's okay. I realized that someone else was a better pal than me. But the sad part is the one who gives it all suffers the most, the other doesn't even get that or even knows that it mattered.

When two people are in love neither of them would know who loves more than the other, however as the relationship progresses one of them would realize that because time and again only one person is taking a back step and letting the other take decisions or compromises on their set of choices most of the time. The one who is compromising the most doesn't even bother mentioning cause he or she is clearly doing this for a reason, and that's because the love for the person matters more than anything else.

So I feel compromises are there in all the relations it's just that the one who compromises the most without complaining clearly loves the most. Not all of them will realize the other person's effort. However, the one who is just exuding love will not even make it look like an effort.

So, let's make an effort towards understanding our people who care, and most importantly let's all stop taking them for granted. Because you may not value the relations when they are with you however, it will leave a vacuum in your life once the same people are not around.

Be the one who is always nice to others, not because they are nice but only because somewhere you are a good person at heart.

You never know today who needs your kindness the most and the ones who actually need, would look like people who are happy anyway. Everyone deserves to be treated well, as much as you do...

57. Look Back Only When You Need To Know How Far You've Come

When I came across this line, I thought to myself, this is so powerful. There's so much that is happening in everyone's life that everyone cannot avoid thinking about the past at all times or think about what's next in store... No one realizes that in the run of dwelling into the thoughts there is so much time that is been wasted.

Every challenge that you have gone through or that you are going through is part of your journey and maybe a part of your learning requirements from life. Take every instance good or bad with a composed thought process so that you react to every situation neutrally.

Just take what is meant to be taken from that situation and move on. Maybe I am sounding like a saint here, but really, being happy at all time is most important. Remember one thing, time is meant to move forward, good or bad it will always pass. No one has the power to hold on to a good time and the best part is neither the bad stays for too long.

One just needs to live in the present moment, only your present situation is of priority; how you are right now, how you feel right now, and what you are doing about your current situation right now, nothing else really matters. You just need to be aware of your current state and need to focus on your next step. The only time you should look back is just to acknowledge how far you've reached and how much you have grown.

I cannot emphasize more how important focusing is. Giving you the simplest example, let's say you are doing one of your office tasks or studying maybe, while you are doing what you are supposed to, you are also thinking about multiple other things that need to be done ahead of the present task or you are thinking about what did not go well yesterday. Here is where you are not able to do justice to your present and neither do you give the right energy and ample time to think about what you were thinking.

Always look at the present and be aware of your future goals.

The way we are built it's important that we look ahead otherwise our eyes would have been at the back of our head. If only looking back was important, we would have walked backward :) Think about it...

58. Conscious You

The more I accentuate on being conscious the more I know I need to work on it. I think everyone cannot be aware of everything that they do all the time. In fact, losing focus is a tendency because there are distractions around us, more so within us. At all times our mind is at constant work; now here's a thing, either you make it work the way you want it to or you work the way it wants you to.

If you want to find a difference in these two phrases, you can find your answer in the results it's giving you, and you'd know what I am talking about.

Everyone talks about being focused in life, being aware; so on and so forth. However, we don't know how to practice it and make it a conscious way of living. Now, most of them would think only people who can meditate for long hours can concentrate. Well, meditation is giving undivided attention to what you want to focus on. It's just telling and training your mind to do one thing at a time and not have all your thoughts scattered.

Here's a way to practice focus; one should give full attention to any task at hand. Whether you are writing something, cleaning your room, getting ready, talking to someone on the phone, or meeting someone personally, whatever the task is you need to give it your full attention. This way you will be training your mind to focus on one thing at a time.

Let's say for example you have three tasks during the day which are critical that need to be attended to immediately and these have been weighing in your mind too much. It would not make sense to be boggled by all three tasks at the same time and not being able to find a solution for either of them. What needs to be done here is, take one task at a time, now when you have one task at hand make sure that you are not thinking about the other two. Your only focus should be what you are currently working on. Take one task at a time and you will be surprised to see the outcome.

Being aware is much underrated, but once you start being conscious of the same, you'd start to notice a lot of things that you may have missed otherwise. A lot of it may require attention but the point is if you do not know what exactly requires to be changed, you will not be able to work on it. Simple things like; what you think, how you behave, the way you react; may require to be looked into and tweaked a bit so that the growth happens for you. Change is all about learning, accepting, and growing, though the first step towards everything is to be conscious of what needs to be done.

A conscious person knows what needs to be spoken before a word is uttered.

59. 2021 almost ending, what changed?

Everyone is excited about the new start to the New Year, because of the way the previous 2 years had been. I guess a larger spectrum of people was affected at the same time. But let me tell you, there may be people who have been suffering from the crisis for the past decade or since the past 5 years, there are also a set of people who did fantastically well in 2020 and 2021, despite the pandemic nothing really affected them. So I think the only difference in these 2 years was the perspective, the way situations were handled, the way new normal was welcomed or criticized.

I am writing this because I am aware that even if the year 2021 is about to get changed nothing changed in the life of many, nothing really changed in the way people think. Because things will change only when you want them to, only if you action them and only if you plan them and analyse if you are working towards what you want. Otherwise, we can keep blaming the situation all our lives, and evidently COVID, the coming year it may be something else or someone else.

We never blame ourselves for our results, that are in a way a feel-good factor. But why don't we get done with taking the onus of it once n for all, just tell yourself "okay! This was where I went wrong and this is where I need correction". Simple right! If we know what needs corrections and where we can make a difference, immediately things can be in our control. Otherwise, we can openly play the blame game all our lives and nothing would change.

Let's be honest to ourselves and be courageous enough to sit down and evaluate, evaluate before it is too late. Mistakes that happen unknowingly can be consciously brought to a solution. But mistakes that one consciously keeps repeating have no solution to it because by then you are comfortable with the results that they are giving you.

Therefore, decide; don't wait for one more year to pass by without you making it slightly better than what you were in the previous year.

60. Unwind... Because it is important

Everything in and around us is moving at a pace, and we are moving along with it to be able to catch up. Sometimes it is important to wait and breathe.

In this continuous rat race where people neither have the time nor the energy to even look at each other, we ought to find time to wait and relax. When you take time to sit back and unwind you are actually doing yourself a favour to be more effective when you start again. It is a process.

Unwinding is important because you need that space for yourself to wait and relax not because you are tired, but because you need to maximize your potential. Even when one exercises one has to take a few seconds to break in between two sets of the same exercise and you all know why you need to do so.

I often used to feel guilty about taking a break from my otherwise busy routine. I thought I may lose my momentum and may not be up to work at the same pace as I did previously. However, when I started to implement the change of focus, it actually got my productivity up to my amazement. We need to always find time to do something that is beside our routine, even if it's a 30-minute stroll. You need to just get that break for yourself.

It is so difficult to empty the mind, there are at all times so many thoughts that your mind is occupied with and sometimes you are not even aware that your mind is overworked. Only when you get those constant headaches or you become irritant in response to the tiniest thing that someone says, you start thinking about what's wrong.

The best way to empty your mind is to put your thoughts on paper and trust me it is a highly underrated act. Try doing this and you will find that you have actually transferred your thoughts on paper and your mind rather is free of unwanted rubbish.

It's like a shift+delete command you give a file that deletes something from your system.

Sleep is another method of unwinding from the routine, however, most of us don't get it enough, most of us have erratic schedules and sleep comes in instalments. A sound sleep of at least 4 hours minimum is a must.

Also, trust that you need your time to rejuvenate and that in any way is not a crime. You absolutely deserve your break. Take one!

61. 21 Century: Where Deleting History Is More Important Than Creating One

With the ohhh sooo complicated world people are behaving furthermore complicated. So much competition to prove oneself, in the run of proving yourself as an intellect, hiding your flaws comes easy than improving yourself.

Why???? Why can't people just be accepting that there are good and bad qualities in them? That the bad only exist in them just because that balances perfection, or let's put it this way in normal terms: NO ONE IS PERFECT.

I have always heard people say, forget the past and start afresh. I kind of disagree with this, though it is not important to constantly be attached to your past. But, the fact of the matter is; you are in your present just because of your past, whatever you have learned, whoever you have met, today the values that you have is just because your past has instilled those in you and that's what has made you.

Of course, you don't need to sink into the negativity of the past but at the same time, you ought to rise from them because of the learning you've had. There is so much out there to be done ahead of you. Essentially, your today will be your past of tomorrow, only if you concentrate well and make your today count, you will be proud of your past in the coming future.

If only more people wake up to the fact that there is an extraordinary person within them who has unlimited potential to do whatever one decides, we would have witnessed so many innovations and wonders around us so far. But because only a few choose to be at the top, and are open to exploring, our overall growth may have been otherwise slow.

Not everyone has a mindset of giving it all to the life they are living, most of them are just satisfied and think achieving more is part of negative greed which one need not have.

"Greedy" is not a bad quality if it may be for knowledge or to be the best of who you can be. It's the way we perceive it.

If I can put it more brutally in words, most of us are too sluggish to get up and get going, and that's precisely a primary reason for someone not giving the best. Nothing can stop anyone to grow unless they are not willing to, and no external support can change that drastically if your will from within is only missing.

I think I have said this before in one of my blogs but I wish to reiterate again, ***We do make our choices, but in the end, our choices make us."***

Strive to create history by working on it today, who knows, you may end up inspiring someone, and manage to change at least one life!

62. Somedays

Somedays, I am just a person who likes to think a million thoughts in a fraction, where so many ideas cluster as multiple lights in my head. And yet I ain't able to find an emotion that defines my reaction to these amazing random ramblings.

Somedays, I am focused as an Arjuna would be on the target. That day passes in a blur before I realize the productivity I've had over my work; I get a sense of accomplishment of the results that just took place.

Somedays, I just want to be, for no reason, I am unknown to myself and how much ever I try to figure out I am not able to understand me, and yet the outer world expects me to unfold my feelings in words, but when I fail to express they think I am closed, rude and at the same time hiding a lot more than I shouldn't.

Somedays, are carefree of the unwanted burden when I weigh-off everything in my head because, I have been somewhere working on myself to not be affected by any external source, subject, or instance.

Somedays, It's cool that way to look carefree even though I may carry a storm inside of me.

Though life happens to everyone; only a few are able to live it fully.

There will be days you will try to figure it out and days where you may not have everything you want. But, you need to know that life is about experiences, everyone is learning and trying to figure it out all this while. None of them has the answer to life, because the moment you think you do, life will change the question…

So I have realized that I need to keep it simple and live in the moment..

Don't waste time to find your answers, they sometimes are meant to find you, don't stop just go on with life… #happylife

63. 11 Things I wish to tell my younger self

Self-talk is funny sometimes, but necessary as hell. There are things you realize while you self talk. It's the clearest form of communication with self, and you cannot help but be honest. Even when you try not to accept certain things, you know what you are refraining from accepting and this is where revelations happen.

There are few things I really wish I knew how to manage, back then but none the less as they say what's meant to be is meant to be. So here are few things that I have learned and may help you relate and implement. Here goes...

1. Don't compare yourself to anyone, because everyone is born unique and your journey is certainly different from anyone else.

2. What you think of yourself is more important than what others think of you. Believe in yourself and trust that no one can know you better than what you know about you.

3. Do not put yourself down and do not give that right to anyone, you are a masterpiece, and your existence counts

4. Be honest to yourself and to others, manipulation of words and actions irks me to the core

5. You will never have control over the results, focus on giving your best, and always remember what did not work for you was never meant for

you. Something better is in store, don't be hassled if things don't work your way. Keep going!

6. People in your life will always come and go, getting attached to people is a tendency, but remember, be as open to letting them go when the time comes or situations demand. Nothing is permanent

7. Time is the most important commodity, spend on things which matter. Don't spend more time being where you'd not want to be, move as soon as you are aware of the same.

8. Be yourself, no one else can be you. You can interpret this one as you like because your perspective matters. However, don't be closed to change, because it will always help you grow.

9. Never ever give up learning; this has to be on-going in your journey. No one is too young or too old to learn.

10. It's never too late to start again, some are billionaires at 26 and some become leaders of a country at 60; everyone has their own timeline. Never say never.

11. Work hard, party with your close people, have deep conversations, love truly, make unique friendships, make your dreams count, respect people, learn to listen, love yourself...

In the end what matters is how you feel about yourself, so as much as you can be happy and keep it simple.

64. Happiness is a State of Mind

Everyone wants to be happy but no one really knows how to keep happy. I think people are trying to find happiness outside, but in reality, happiness is just hidden within us.

There are so many articles, blogs, videos that people go through when they are not in their so-called good mood. Everyone is searching for external sources that they think will keep them happy. However, what one doesn't realize is that they fail to implement what would lead them to change their state of mind.

Today's trends are moving towards being very extremely reactive in everything that one experiences. For example: If a person suffers from mild cough and fever in these times, they would immediately think that they might have caught COVID, without even having second thoughts of it being any other correlation to their medical complaints. It could be viral or just another mild infection that they otherwise may have caught.

Such extreme thinking leads to running the mind in random directions and putting your energy in things that only your mind creates.

It becomes way too easy if one takes everything at the face value and doesn't try reading between the lines. When you take situations, people, and life as is, only then it will become easy to go by your days and take one day at a time and one moment at a time.

If only everyone understood the simple fact that every situation has a solution we wouldn't spend our time thinking of the adverse possibilities that may occur. Instead, I feel everyone should only focus on things that are in their control and leave the rest of it for life to take over, trust me it will never fail you.

Everything happens for a reason, you need to keep your calm because everything that is happening in and around you is teaching you something.

Happy doesn't only mean partying and dancing to loud music or going out for a drink with friends, it can also mean to sit on a porch with your closest pal, facing the sea, speaking no word at all and still walking back home thinking that was the best conversation you've ever had.

Everyone's idea of happiness differs from the other. Happiness is a state of mind; most of them are mistaken trying to find it only in the external form.

Like everything else that we have learnt so far, I think learning to be happy needs to be well practised.

65. Mind Chatter

It's amazing how the mind works. Everyone thinks that the mind never gets tired as it is supposed to be constantly at work. But what we don't understand is that it has it's unwind time, that's the time when it enjoys being in a space that gives happy vibes. When you do things you like or which you are passionate about, that's the actual mind space it enjoys.

So many people complain of not being able to speak their mind or not being able to convey their thoughts into words, that's because there is clutter in their mind already which doesn't let them convey effectively. Most of them don't even realize that they are over-thinkers, if you notice these are also people who speak fast or don't speak at all. They try to get done with what they want to speak because there are series of thoughts they need to attend to or they are not able to focus on what needs to be spoken and rather choose to keep mum.

Most of the over-thinkers who are not doing anything to manage their thoughts have a lot of adverse effects in the long run. A lot of times when they get feedback of overthinking or speaking really fast, they tend to get conscious of themselves.

No one knows how to manage the mind, however, there are so many things available today that are constantly advising you on ways of controlling the mind. However, the first step towards managing your mind is to accept the fact that you are an over-thinker and you need to change that. Once you accept this you will be open to whatever needs to be done to change that.

Learn to focus, that is the primary way of diverting your mind towards something that you want to focus on. Train your mind to do what you want it to; do not work according to what the mind demands from you. When you start doing this, it acts as an exercise for you to build your mind-muscle, just like you exercise your body. However, the results don't take place overnight; it has to be a constant effort and a consistent one.

A lot of people are prisoners to their thoughts, they can easily get caged and not come out of it for days. This is where it gets uncontrollable. Only when you want to get out, would you put enough effort to change things for yourself. Else, this will just be on-going, and before you realize it will be too late to take corrective measures.

When your mind talks to you, ensure that it's a healthy conversation that you would enjoy and which helps you to take the next best step.

Blessed are those who enjoy their own company, and I am sure of these conversations to be enriching ones. Only a healthy environment for your mind will create a healthy thought process...

66. Journey of an entrepreneur is alone

Today with the times changing everyone is looking to do something different and become successful. Entrepreneurship is on everyone's mind these days. However, does one understand the weight it has on the shoulders?

All want a fancy life but none are ready to pay the price for the prize that it has in store for you. Very few are ready for the journey. Some question themselves and some waste time in thinking if it is actually meant for them.

A decision is what it takes to do anything and everything in life.

When I say a decision it doesn't merely mean a decision it means being committed to the decision you have taken. And doing what is necessary to walk on this journey.

If you look around anything that you do requires the same amount of commitment from your end, what matters is how serious are you about it. Be it changing a habit, getting in shape, working on a relationship, making friends, taking care of family, etc., anything and everything requires you to take that decision in terms of following certain things. If you don't follow you will fall short of being able to give it all and eventually the results definitely wouldn't match your goals.

Gathering yourself is the first step, then asking yourself if it is worth the commitment and the most important making a promise to stick by it. If you think you will not be able to do justice in either of the three then you should not think about stepping into it in the first place. Because, once you are there you are there in that space, and if you are not able to give what it demands from you, it may not be a happy feeling, or rather you will re-think the decision.

You have to remember that this journey is your own and only you can train yourself, of course, if you have a great mentor it will help you get there. But again, motivation is like having a bath, it has to be a daily practice otherwise you will again be back to square one.

There are two things one can do here, 1- submit yourself fully to your source or your mentor who is guiding you and, 2- make yourself strong enough to not be distracted by your surroundings.

The mind is a wanderer by nature, if you don't train it to focus it will make you a slave. If you train it well; you will be the best master it ever can have.

Only you are capable of making or breaking your life, choose wisely and success will choose you.

67. Few Quotes that I stumbled upon, today are affixed to my brain like tattoos

We all love to read quotes, especially those which we relate to, and some of them just stay with us. No matter how much you try to, we never forget them. Time and again they keep reminding you that they exist and you cannot really help but know, how much they make you think rather how they make you feel.

Here goes…

1. ***Books serve to show a person that those original thoughts of his aren't very new after all:***

As I said something that quotes do to you is make you realize that what you thought was not really thought by you alone, it universally exists. Books give you an open world that exposes your mind to a million thoughts and perspectives that you already had or you never thought of. Sometimes you are so surprised that the writers are exactly putting your mind into words. I love the way some books are capable of taking you to places you've never been before and that's the beauty of words that are combined with energy.

2. ***Not all those who wander are lost:***

This quote taught me that a wandering mind need not always be lost. Some people are deep thinkers and most of the fantastic ideas and thoughts have come into perspective because of these wanderers. However one should be aware of one's state of mind, only those who know how to control their mind can control their thoughts

3. *I love you not for what you are, but for what I am when I am with you:*

Well…This quote is really close to me. I always feel that when you really like someone you like them because they change something in you. It is always the way their presence makes you feel. You tend to discover a lot of things about you that you otherwise wouldn't. Love is really very powerful, and it is applicable to all the relations in life. If you see for yourself, the relations that you have maintained until today with people and the ones you will maintain in the future is just because somewhere there is love involved. If there was no love involved it's just there for a purpose or an agenda that will fizzle out when the purpose is met.

4. *I fell in love like we fall asleep, slowly and all at once:*

This is a quote from "The fault in our stars" and I just fell in love with this quote because somewhere I related to this one. It just talks volumes about how one falls into love. I feel the faster one falls into love the faster some may fall out of love as well, but I also think to each is its own. I don't believe in love at first sight, because I haven't had that experience yet. However, I strongly feel that it is the bond or vibe that one feels more than the attraction. Once you vibe right, I guess everything else falls in place or rather may just feel right. Perfection is all about being imperfectly perfect for your imperfectly perfect person.

5. ***Life gives answers in three ways: it says Yes and gives it to you, it says No and gives you something better, it says wait and gives you the best in your lifetime:***

This is the quote I live with, I always believe, what you lost or did not get wasn't meant for you anyway, so keep finding your right. Sometimes what you ask for is less than what you deserve and that's when the universe takes time to give you what you deserve. Most of us fail to believe the fact that **time** is what it takes to be where we want to be, we are in a rush to get what we want and when the delay happens we lose trust. I think having patience in everything that we do is very important because we all have a timeline and when the time is right we will get what we deserve. I totally trust the master plan, It has always filled my life with amazing things and opportunities. Some of them I never thought I deserved, but today I am grateful for them...

6. ***The harder we fall the faster we get up:***

This quote I have heard from my fav Bollywood actor, Shahrukh Khan (I am an ardent fan). We all think about the hardships and challenges that we are put through and we always think of these two words "WHY ME". But have you really thought about your journey, if you notice clearly, only these challenges have made you the person you are today. Everyone grows out of the challenges; and when they do, they come out stronger. So always know that whatever you are put through, you are very much capable of tackling the situation otherwise you wouldn't have been there in the first place. You are stronger than you think you are!

7. ***When God pushes you to the edge of difficulties, only two things happen. Either he will hold you when you fall or teach you how to fly.***

I can't even tell you what this quote means to me in words. All I can just say or maybe sum it up in one word **"FAITH'.**

68.   Self Importance: A Massive Burden

As much as they say that first help yourself and then help others in need, this is very true. However, there is a very thin line between putting yourself first and making yourself important. Self-importance is more of a burden, I think because people are loaded with the ego of it. It is important to feel important but not at the cost of demeaning others. Instead of making necessary changes within themselves towards improvement, people tend to put others down.

Most of the arguments, sour relations, and meaningless exchange of words happen because of self-importance. If you look closely at why you reacted the way you did, you would realize that you could have reacted differently if you kept aside only an individual perspective and looked at an overall scenario.

Everyone has a right to choose their set of right or wrong as you do, so if their right doesn't match yours, it is okay. It is just their choice. For example when you are not invited to a particular party you feel bad / left out etc. A lot of them feel that things should go as you want them to, but believe me, there is some power that definitely knows what suits you better.

Of course our existence matters, but always think about an overall point of view. Sometimes giving more importance to yourself than the situation may not allow you to look at things from the other's point of view.

Only when one is open to considering someone else's thoughts, will there be a lot to learn. Growth is certain when one is ready to receive, but the one who just doesn't want to budge from what he/she thinks is right will lose on to a chance of growth.

Knowing that others are as important as you, treating your surrounding as you want to be treated, giving an ear, and listening with full attention is very important

A lot can change around you if you think about others as well.

No relation gets stronger without love and respect. Love others as you love yourself and as you may want others to respect you.

69.   8 Simple things that help you take care of your body

Taking care of your body is very essential and today there are so many things available outside that claim to be good. However, there can be simple things in your routine that can help you to take care of yourself so that you reside in a healthy environment of your healthy body.

Here are few steps that one can do to keep your body healthy

1. **Rest well:** Resting these days comes in instalments, people are so overworked with no productivity that they tend to complain of a lot of lethargicness, body ache, and tiredness. The primary reason for these complaints is that the body is not rested enough. A good night's sleep is the most important part of your rest. Ensure you have no phone around you to distract your sleep. The moment you are close to your sleep time you need to put all your work away and only rest.

2. **Shower:** A good warm shower in the morning freshens you up to kick start your day and the same shower at night puts you to sound night sleep. It's amazing that doing the same thing at two different timings can give you different results. Adding rock salt to your bathing water helps. Rock salt is rich in minerals and warm water helps your body absorb the minerals better

3. **Keep yourself hydrated:** Drinking enough water is very essential for your body. Our body comprises 70 percent of water and it needs to

fulfil the water requirement of the day. Drinking at least 2–3 litres is important (unless otherwise recommended by your medical practitioner). It keeps your skin plump, keeps your hair moisturized, keeps your system intact, helps proper digestion.

4. **Exercise:** Do any form of exercise that you like,even if it is just a stroll for 30 minutes. Exercising helps better the blood circulation and keeps your energy levels high and refreshed

5. **Eat well:** Eating proper food is very very important. There is a saying "you are what you eat". So if you eat only junk food, you will look like a bag full of chips ;). Of course, you can have your days where you can let yourself easy. Ensure at least 80 percent of the time you watch what you eat. It will help you know where you can add healthy options

6. **Spend time with yourself:** Have at least one hour to yourself. Each day ensure you spend time with yourself and be aware of your thoughts. In the clutter of what is happening around you, rarely would you find time for yourself. You need to align with yourself and as much as you can in that one-hour focus on what you want. A healthy mind will always result in a healthy body environment and vice a versa

7. **Listen to your body:** At all times your body speaks with you. For example when you feel thirsty that's the body's signal that you have not had enough water. If you drink water at regular intervals you wouldn't feel thirsty. Also, some people who go on diets may have an urge someday to have a proper meal; at that time you ought to listen to what your body is asking you need the nourishment to sustain the energy in

the body. Not everyone will react similarly to the same kind of food. Some may also lose weight by eating carbs and some may put on with complex carbs as well.

8. **Avoid Synthetic products:** There are so many products available in the market telling you that you get better skin or healthy hair and so on and so forth. As much as you can, stick to nature based products. Being in India is a blessing as there are so many things available easily which contribute to great health. Ghee (clarified butter) is very underrated for the benefits it provides, including one spoon of ghee in your diet makes your skin supple and moisturized. Oiling your hair regularly helps your hair to stay hydrated even if you are using a shampoo that has tonnes of chemicals. A combination of Castor oil and Coconut oil (1:3 ratio) is a blessing for your hair, it also promotes hair growth. Dates, green leafy vegetables, white butter, flax seeds, sunflower seeds, walnuts, black raisins, all these products are packed with nutrients. Include them in your routine (in moderation) and you will find a lot of improvement in your overall health.

This is not a regime I wish everyone to follow, however, these are things that I have included and have seen the visible difference and therefore have listed them down. In case of any medical condition please consult a professional before following, especially the 7th and 8th point since it is very subjective.

70. Get Inspired And Keep Going

Are you inspired? When did you check on your level of inspiration last? Also, what keeps you going everyday.

Everyone needs that one inspiration in their life which makes them get up in the morning and get going. However, if you think the inspiration in your life is missing you ought to find it. I feel everything that I do / will do or have done is because I was inspired to do so, either by myself or by some situation or someone who influenced me.

I think finding an influence that keeps you on your toes each day is like finding a goal to live, it just keeps you on track. Otherwise, you will see time pass by with no productivity to it. You may at certain times, have happened to just watch your day just pass by, which leads you to think why haven't you utilized your time well. Or, you may at times think your day could have been better. Well, happens with everyone, but the point is, are you correcting it the next time.

Your life influences and choices make you who you are today, somewhere you are a mixture of your learning and your influences that you have had in your life. The best thing to do is surrounding yourself with people who love you and who want you to grow in life and with whom you learn from every day. These things if included in your routine you will find a difference in the way you function each day.

The problem is most of us are too lazy to find an influence or a purpose because of the fear of commitment. Once you decide to walk the path you need to be committed to it, and that's where most of us lack. However, people who have continued to walk the path despite the negative voice in their heads have converted their commitment into a habit.

Always be the one who is inspired every day, someday you will influence a lot of people to change the way they function...

Let the influences in you have the power to inspire and lighten up someone else's life...

71. Are you Creating more than you consume???

What I mean to refer to here is that we often are consuming so much of the information around us that we are merely taking any notice of what it is trying to teach us. Knowledge is only made of appropriate use when it is implemented otherwise, knowledge that is neither exchanged nor implemented just stays as information that one has.

Everyone today is so busy that when they want to take a break or move their mind from their routine; often find social media, video games, movies, etc as their favorite pass time or unwinding weapon. There are very few who choose to sketch, playing an instrument, writing, etc as their go-to stress buster. People have stopped creating. They only consume what is around them and that is just what it is.

Somewhere creativity has lost its importance I would say because the idea of passing time has a different meaning altogether.

The mind is the most important they say, but I think that mind needs to be trained by you. Everything that needs to be perfected requires thorough practice and so does the mind.

Be aware of what you are doing and you will know how much time you are spending doing something which has no productive outcome. If you choose your tasks wisely and have a timeline, there is much more you can do with the time at hand. Otherwise, you will only complain about not having enough time.

We are built to be creative and we need to explore our creative side to be able to tap the yet unknown.

72. Silence Has More Words Than An Actual Conversation Would Ever Have

Being silent doesn't define the weakness of a person, it rather says a lot about the person's patience. Most of them tend to talk a lot when it comes to emoting or putting across something, however, if you notice, sometimes an otherwise talkative person may just go quiet to avoid conflicts.

Sometimes being quiet not only helps to avoid unfavourable responses but also gives you time to think before you speak. Because, when you react instantly, you may sometimes regret certain words spoken which are too late to be taken back.

Some people when they go silent appear strangely dangerous because they really cook a response and get back with multi-fold energy.

Never underestimate the power of silence. It has the power to avoid the worst but at the same time, it has the power to create a swirl of thoughts in the minds of others.

For me, Silence is all about expression. I am silent when I am not comfortable with the company. I am silent when I don't want to utter words that may hurt others. I am silent when I am thinking deeply. I am silent when I am listening and observing things and people around me. I am silent when words fall short for me to express, I am silent when I want to express hurt or love.

I tend to stay silent at significant moments. Though, I am yet to explore what goes into my head when I am completely silent, suddenly in the midst of a conversation, which again I will figure out when I am focusing on myself / meditating in silence.

It's amazing what being quiet can do to you. Learning to enjoy your silence as much as you enjoy conversations can raise a level of intellect in you.

I have replaced Words of Wisdom with, Space of Silence.. (well that's original)

73. Somethings are better said and some are better left unsaid

All of us carry a lot of thoughts in our minds, these also include judgments of other people and situations. Often, we wonder how would it be if we confide in someone or share our perspective of an instance with the actual person to whom it needs to be addressed. However, we are left perplexed whether to confess or not just because we are scared about the repercussion of the disclosure.

Situations land us into moments where we don't know whether to talk our minds or just be diplomatic so that the person listening to us doesn't feel bad. We do realize what words can do and therefore most of the time we tamper our thoughts and choose the right set of words just because we need to behave civilized or we do not want to create a swirl of heated conversations and majorly protect the relationship.

Most of the time, it is always best to not reply at the spur of the moment and talk about it when everything settles so that there can be a mature discussion that can lead to a favorable outcome.

As much as it is important to speak your mind and get it out of your system, sometimes keeping quiet and completely ignoring what you had to say would be a better option. This happens when you know if you spoke your mind you may spoil your relation with the person. Also, this needs to be weighed in particular, even before you utter any words. Firstly, understand what is more important, the person or the situation, sometimes you don't need a right or wrong.

However, when you choose to keep quiet, you need to ensure to drop the entire thought so that it does not affect you or your future conversations. Because, this may unknowingly change your behaviour towards that person.

Work on yourself to be able to rise above everything else and always look at everything around you as is, without any baggage of the past and without any filter in your eyes.

Understand that people are more important than situations, but also know that you have a choice of choosing your self-respect over someone's behavior, and that line can only be drawn by you.

74. Understanding People

Often we tend to understand people our way; we don't even try to understand their perspective. We mostly never treat them the way they are, we treat them as we think they are. Only constant communication will allow you to understand them better.

Also, everyone has a basic nature, some open up the moment they meet people, some take their time to open up and understand the other person before putting themselves out there. On the other hand, some are plain introverts they would only communicate when someone puts an effort to communicate; otherwise, they are okay being by themselves.

People are different and not everyone would get along with everyone, you tend to have your comfort level with some of them, and with some, you only wish to keep it short. There may be no wrong in being that way.

Sometimes you may encounter instances in life where you are forced to communicate with people you do not like to communicate with, however in this case most of them generally try to break the ice just so they try to keep the communication on and manage the person just the way they are.

A major example of this is a joint family, people living in joint families may not necessarily get along with each other, but they tend to find a midway where everyone stays happy. It is practically not possible for a person to get along with everybody, however, one can just accept people at the face value. This not only makes it easy for the relationship to sustain but keeps the unwanted friction at bay.

In wanting people to understand us more we fail to understand them better, I think the first step towards having an expectation from someone is fulfilling an expectation, which means if I expect something from someone, there might be a possibility of someone else expecting the same out of me.

So treat everyone the way you want to be treated.

75. Habits That Are Underrated

It takes ages for us to cultivate habits and these habits further to become our way of life. However, there are few habits that have been important in our heads but highly devalued when it comes to implementing these in our routine.

Here goes...

1. **Having time for yourself**: In the rush of your daily work that you have to go by, one forgets to have time for self. "I don't have enough time" is the phrase that is commonly used by most. Though I think one does not realize the importance of giving time to self. By giving time I mean pausing your routine to see what is your day's plan or maybe checking on how has your day been. Make time for yourself either at the start of your day or at the end of the day. Depending on the time you decide, ensure this time as an opportunity to just be by yourself and think about what you feel. Because unless you feel happy about what you do or have been doing you will not enjoy the process of reaching where you want to be. Also, this space can be utilized to just know about yourself more and let yourself be in your control. If you and your thoughts are in control you will have better control of your day.

2. **Your To-Do list**: This really sounds like a cliché, but a to-do list is a must-have. This list is so underrated that even if one wants to decide to start making it, one would think I can remember everything. I think a to-do list is more of a self-note so that one gets a sense of direction for the

day and knows what the tasks are that one needs to accomplish during the day. It's amazing how satisfying it is to tick done against a task when you get through with them one at a time.

3. **Being surrounded by people you love**: It's amazing how your company can change your energy. It's highly important to be around people who think good about you and for you. It helps you have a good vibe. The best part is when you work or spend most of the time with such a crowd your growth aspects just rise muti-fold. You are just in the right mindset and are open and encouraged to do well. If you check yourself, your mood is directly proportional to the company you are in at that point in time. Also if you feel you have not been in the right energy off late, immediately check your company and possibly change your circle as fast as you can.

4. **Reading**: Now I know most of them would think, they are not the people who read books at all. But trust me, one has to adapt a taste to read. Once you do, you open doors to a vast set of knowledge and perspective. It amazes me the amount of experiences that people have been through has been put into words so beautifully. It's a world of words that can change your life literally.

5. **Listening more**: Everyone has opinions and communication these days have become competitive, everyone wants to be ready with their set of answers and their set of opinions. Where, one is only listening to answer back and not willing to actually listen to the perspective of the other person. It is very important to listen before we speak. When you give an ear to someone's thought would someone be open to listening to you. It works like respect; you never

ask for it, you need to respect people first to get respected. In a conversation, the one who listens to understand would be able to share a favorable and relevant response, as well as has a vast chance of learning new perspectives.

76. Your State Of Mind

Your current state of mind determines the quality of your day. Often everyone is driven by their current mental state, but no one tries to maintain a happy state of mind. Instead of the circumstances driving our mind, we need to train our mind to be composed and detached.

I have learned this word somewhere "Demotional" which means detached from emotions. One has to practice being practical most of the time. It is very easy to make emotion-based decisions in life. But let me be also practical by saying it is not easy to leave emotions aside all the time, the least you can do is change your focus and self-talk, it does help.

A mind is software that needs to be programmed in a certain manner; the more you run the program the more you become better at it. Being able to practice a state of mind is an achievement in itself and perfecting it makes you the master of your mind.

I have come across people who are so composed that their reaction is very neutral even when extremely happy or extremely sad, I just find them consuming the emotion and dealing with it. Such people are able to channelize themselves and focus on whatever they want to at any given point, just because they are not driven by their minds.

I have most of the time taken my bad mood as an excuse for not being able to focus on work and therefore let the day pass without any productivity. Now sometimes it is essential for you to feel the emotion you are dealing with but most of the time even if you know you can overcome that low feeling by changing your focus, you still want to lean on your bad mood to have a break from the routine.

It is only you who can decide what is more important, you can either immerse yourself with millions of excuses, feeling why are things not going the way you want them to or just find one reason to ensure you do whatever it takes to have things moving for you. No one has escaped bad situations in life, but what you think and do on your bad days will determine how much your bad days will last.

Optimism is knowing that everything happens for good, and strength lies in facing everything despite all the odds. Life otherwise is a beautiful piece of art, you will not know what the picture looks like till you draw your last stroke.

77. Emotion Composure

What do you do when you are at your lowest point? Have you observed your pattern when you are off because of a bad day at work or in your personal life? Emotions are needed to be felt, however, what each needs is to get away with the odd feeling so that one can find ways and means to feel better.

I think that people ought to feel their lows in order to appreciate their highs. Also, one needs to know why they feel in a certain manner to be able to understand themselves more. It, therefore, becomes easy to understand why one has been reacting or feeling in a certain manner. Mind and heart perceives every information differently and hence everyone responds to it differently.

Learn to have a composed reaction to everything that you experience, of course, this would happen through practice. However, do not stop yourself from experiencing and expressing what you are feeling. There is a reason why we experience emotions

Everyone is going through their ups and downs, it is a pattern in everyone's life. The point is how you behave at your lows and how much it affects you.

It is important to be able to reach a state of composure and to be able to manage yourself when you are in the midst of getting over your low and moving towards your normal state. If you are taking days to get back to a positive state of mind then you need to practice changing your focus and be aware of your thoughts.

There is a vast difference between when you control your thoughts and when your thoughts control you. Do not let the mind control what you need to think, train your mind to think differently and you will be astonished by the results. You may have heard this a lot of times — "Our mind is an excellent slave but a bad master."

Why operate your energy to a lower frequency when you have the power to operate at a higher frequency and attract all the good things that you want and deserve.

Your quality of thoughts define your quality of life.

78.   Know What You Want

It is very important to be very clear about everything that you do, perceive or plan to achieve. Without clarity moving ahead becomes baseless. Would you ever leave your house without knowing why are you stepping out? Or would you call for food without knowing what you want to order? You wouldn't right! Then why do we lead our lives without having clarity of thoughts? Did you ever think about it?

Often, we go by our day just finishing our daily work and get lost in our routines for days and weeks together not knowing where are we heading towards. Our respective careers do that with us, for months together we are following targets and goals of our organizations without working on our own goals.

Or let me put it this way, our organization goals somewhere become our goals and our way of life, there is nothing left to do for ourselves because there is no time left.

Time and again we need to look at ourselves and our progress; financial and career progress is not the only growth prospects to focus on. You need to add to your learning every single day. Work on your focus areas, take time to follow your passion, spend time with yourself, take care of your health, spend time with family, and, most of all work on what you want.

Spend time to think and write what you exactly want in life, what makes you happy, and work on the betterment of the quality of your life, rather than just leading it like driftwood.

Knowing what you want is a power everyone should have, so you can direct your life as you want and not depend on situations to change.

Change yourself and you will see situations change which will further change the results. Take control of your life well in advance, because no one else will do that for you.

Of course, life is unpredictable, but being in control of yourself will teach you a lot about yourself and will help you manage situations that come your way. #happylife

79. Power of Decision making

Well, I call it a power of decision-making because it is definitely a POWER that we possess. One doesn't realize the impact that a decision could make in our life. We all keep making small and big decisions every day, which unknowingly may bring about a major change or shift in our lives.

Today, whatever we are and wherever we are is the result of the decisions that we've made over the period of time, these decisions may have compelled us to make necessary changes in our life, where some changes were swiftly made and some really took time for us to absorb into our routine.

Whatever the decisions maybe it is we who have to make them. However, our external environment tends to influence our decision-making, and therefore, we are flummoxed as to what needs to be done.

I have always in such situations, weighed down all the thoughts that creep in due to the external environment and mostly go according to what my gut says. I have witnessed that laying down pros and cons helps to take a calculative decision. But, I have come to a conclusion that most of my decisions are based on how I feel at that point in time, whatever my gut feeling says I take that leap of faith. Trust me, it hasn't failed me.

Also, I feel the only reason one becomes indecisive is due to the fear of results.

Never think about the results, as results can change because efforts are under our control.

We all at some point have to take decisions, they may be right or wrong, none are so godly that can always take or gauge if the decision is right. One should arrive at a decision and make it right. It's our life, after all, let's be responsible enough to take our decisions and be ready to get on with the consequences coming our way.

For most of them, wrong decisions have been a major learning curve. And it has been these wrong decisions why people have always appreciated the right ones.

It is very important to take responsibility, ownership, and control of our lives. Our life will not always be the way we plan, as much as it sounds scary; it gives us an edge of adventure to enjoy. It's simply the way we look at it.

Sometimes we Succeed and other times we Learn...

80. Thoughts in Control

Do you control your thoughts or your thoughts control you (read that again) People are full of emotions some know how to emote and some make a failed attempt to control them.

However most of the time everyone seems more flummoxed on how one needs to react to a particular situation or how one can be in control of themselves.

Firstly, understand that, be it good or bad emotion both are meant to be felt. Not necessarily one needs to react to them, but one needs to be definitely aware of how certain things make them feel. Second of all, however tempting it may be, one should not react at that moment. Thirdly one needs to be aware of the time that one spends thinking. If you are affected by something of course you would take your time getting out of it but, it is also equally important to not be swayed completely and not being aware of the unnecessary time that you spend immersed in the thought.

Change your focus as soon as you can and find your favorite task to work on, doing what you like will change the way you feel. If you observe your routine carefully, you will notice that the days you had a happy feeling from the time you woke up were the days that went well and the day something made your mood miserable at the very start of the day, that day surprisingly everything went literally opposite of what you wanted it to be. There is no surprise to this actually, this happens because the energy within and around you reflects; happy will always attract happy, and otherwise.

You therefore always like to be around people who have happy energy, no one likes to be around people who always complain or who always have that negative vibe going on.

Ensure that you are the one who is in control of your thoughts and your responses, change the way you feel and you will see things change around you...

We are blessed to be able to understand and deliver emotions, unlike other living beings. Let's appreciate the fact that this is so much better than not being able to express at all. #happylife

81. Communication Can Open Doors

Communication is an important tool, one needs to know how to communicate clearly. Words can say a lot and one needs to be very careful while they choose what they say and ensure that they're putting across what they feel.

It's amazing what a conversation can do, it can build a relationship for life or it can loosen a bond. However, people communicate more to manage perceptions than make others understand their true selves.

When you ensure that you are honest in what you speak, and the intent is right the opposite person will get the energy and trust in what you say. Though it should be both ways, a one-way communication will still fail if the other is not making any effort.

Every lasting relation has one thing in common, they don't die out of words to communicate. If you can communicate endlessly with someone it's the best kind of bond, be it your mom, dad, siblings, friends, spouse, or relatives.

If you are not able to communicate what you feel, people tend to assume things and you don't want that. If you want to be understood, make it easy for others by communicating well. Of course, once you converse more you know a person more, and then unspoken words also can be understood. However, it all starts with talking, the more you speak the more you understand, and the more you can be understood.

Help people understand you better by putting your thoughts into words, undisclosed words may not necessarily convey what you exactly want to.

Therefore,

Want to express yourself- Speak

Want to confront someone- Speak

Want to apologize for something that you think might hurt the other person- Speak

Want to tell someone you were hurt- Speak

Want any advice- Speak

Want to make someone understand your side- Speak

In short, at all times you need to express it through words.

Man invented language to communicate, let's keep it that way. Simple!

82. Loving Unconditionally

What does loving unconditionally actually mean? It means that a person loves someone without expectation. It means that whether or not the opposite person feels the same way, one continues to give without wanting anything in return.

But does such love exist in today's world? Well, it absolutely does exist, however, the "UNCONDITIONAL" is losing its value cuz it's been used rather cheaply by people without realizing its worth.

The purest form of unconditional love is of the mother and the child, where the mother does not expect anything in return and continues to give her unwavering attention, love, and care to the child.

Love is a language that has the power to heal, whether spoken or expressed it conveys what it needs to when done with good intent.

However, I feel sometimes people lack gratefulness and therefore fail to acknowledge the ever-giving nature of people around them; be it friends, family, partner, spouse, siblings, etc. And that's when I think everyone should draw a line as to how much one should keep putting effort into.

There is a very thin line between intent and self-respect; your intent may be genuine but one should also know that if the opposite person doesn't value the effort put in, one should know when to stop.

Stay away from people who will only want you to be around when they need you. Of course with the busy schedule, everyone cannot give ample amount of time to each other. But, If one cares enough one will make time and effort, remember that. There is nothing like "I don't have time." It is just about setting priorities right.

If it is important enough they will make time, or you move away. Simple!

Though unconditional implies not setting any expectations, however, you should know who is deserving of your unconditional love.

Love unconditionally but also know when it is not valued.

83. What is your ideal life?

Did anyone ask you this question before? If you ever had to define your ideal life what would it be like and who do you want to be around.

At some point, everyone has imagined what they want or what they wouldn't want as a part of their routine in bits and pieces. You've always gone about having this thought and forgetting about it. And trust me, the problem is not wanting the best of what we can; but it lies in forgetting about what we want.

Routines are so set that you tend to get comfortable in your own rut. Not necessarily it is your favourite way of living your life, but you tend to make peace with yourself that this is what it is, and nothing more can be achieved or changed.

What if whatever you have always dreamt of comes true! By whatever I literally mean whatever... Just imagine!!!! Your favourite destination travel, a nice big villa, healthy family and you surrounded by amazing friends, partying whenever you feel like, taking a break and flying to the most favourite holiday destination whenever you want to. Not being bound by duties officially, and most of all working on your passion project. How easy and fun life would have been. The thought of it only makes you feel happy right?!

But just because we stop reliving this dream again and again in our minds and hearts we tend to forget about it. A dream should become a guiding force that doesn't put you to rest until you are where you have always wanted to be. I think we have started settling for too little and that's where the problem lies.

As Steve Jobs says "Never Settle" keep going until you find what you want.

What you deserve will find its way towards you only when you make an effort to walk towards it. Energy attracts energy. Without you putting in an equal amount of effort you wouldn't get the results that you desire.

Dream about your ideal life and one day you will live it for real, keep working towards it. You already know what needs to be done, let's start putting it to action.

84. Now is a Perfect time!

We all wait for that perfect time always. Let's say for example I will start exercising once my routine gets a bit easy; I will start waking up early from next month onward; I will start saving up once I start earning say an "X amount". But none knows when would that perfect time arrive, and also once it does your wants change, you look forward to a different excuse altogether. This is a vicious circle, it will never end until we put an end to it.

Most of the time we are scared to do what we want because maybe we are too comfortable in our routine, maybe we are too hesitant to make that shift to be a little uncomfortable, and maybe we are avoiding getting into a commitment and that's why we never really start.

Fear of not being able to commit gets in a way of doing something that we really want to do or what may help us become better. However, we all somewhere need to understand that some things take that extra effort (pain) for us to get better (gain) and that's why they say no Gain without Pain.

Have you ever seen someone who is really well-spoken, or well built, or intellectually so informed about most of the subjects; do you think that comes naturally? Not really, everyone has to work on themselves to be able to be the best. The point is we will never be able to see the effort behind someone's expertise, we only see the changed version of someone and appreciate thinking that may have come easy for that person but for you, it would be difficult.

Everything in life needs to be worked on, so much so that there comes a day when it seems effortless.

Most of us keep that special dress for the special occasion, wear that amazing smelling perfume for that one perfect day, save a fortune to travel one day to that one particular favourite holiday destination. Why wait for that one perfect time, when you can enjoy your moment today.

Do what you want to do today, work for something you want to achieve today, wear that special dress today, because there will always be a better perfect time ahead of you, but your "best perfect is now!

START... Before it's too late, and start NOW because there is no perfect time then right now.

85. "Mood Swings" an unfamiliar territory

We all have our mood swings good, bad, and ugly. Sometimes we do know why they exist and sometimes we ourselves don't figure out why we are behaving in a particular manner. In fact, we also voice it out to ourselves "Why am I behaving like that, this is so not me".

Often we fail to understand ourselves and we wish we knew how to tackle our mood in those times. It's very ironic that these are the times we wish others understood us, and this is where we expect too much from the outer world.

It is good to have people who know you and who are there to handle your mood swings though, but as painful as it is for you to go through those mood swings imagine what the person on the receiving end must be going through.

Do you think it's easy for the other person to understand you then? Not really, but if the other person is making it look easy, then never let go of such a person from your life.

Introspection is what you need to do when you don't know what is bothering you. Often, you know the reason behind your mind's chaos it's just that sometimes you need to address it to yourself very clearly. And when you do, you need to find a favorable solution. Once the solution happens it's no more a concern.

And what if there's no solution to your problem? I say if there's no solution then why bother thinking about it, just leave it as is and you will see that the universe will take care of it.

It's worth waiting for things to unfold on their own and keep your anxiety at bay.

You don't need to know everything. Sometimes, not knowing answers is actually good for your peace of mind. Also, what you need to know you already know or you will know in time.

Just go on with life and "do what you know you want to do"...

86. Reactions are not meant to hurt others so watch when you react

We often tend to react swiftly; let's just say that we are quite unaware of how much weight our reactions have until we unknowingly hurt someone with one of these impulsive responses.

We do know that sometimes we do not have control on our own reactions, but barely are aware and cautious of the same.

Imagine someone joking about something which you are very sensitive about, you'd feel hurt right. Though people do not vocalize it up front as they may also know it was not meant the way it was said, however, at the same time when people are hurt such thoughts sit in their head for a while. This depends on how grave the topic was, the intensity of the hurt caused may vary accordingly.

People these days are very closed, everyone is kind of fighting their own battle. I think the kind of schedule that everyone has and the kind of expectations that are built around have made everyone very discrete. Sharing has become more filtered, and therefore you wouldn't know if you actually know a person fully. People like to be in their own shell and deal with their own sh*t by themselves.

Everything is changing around you constantly and of course this will have an impact on you somewhere or the other. With everything changing you need to take charge and responsibility of the change that takes place within you and here is where **awareness** plays a major role.

Everyone cares, everyone needs an ear, everyone has an emotional side, everyone is sensitive towards something close to them. Therefore being cautious of what we say and how we react is more important.

Empathy is a rare quality; it has to be practiced to be mastered. Put yourself in the other person's shoes even before you react. They say wrong words can be swords, but wrong reactions can be sharper.

Watch yourself in your head first before someone else gets to see you react.

87. Fascinated by tomorrow? Watch what you doing now!

We have always been fascinated by the next opportunity, the next big break, the next steps, and the next achievement. But sometimes I think if we're thinking way ahead and losing the opportunity of enjoying our today.

We tend to think about tomorrow, if you don't believe me let me give you an example. Think how you feel on a Friday evening when you are just about to get into your weekend and then think about how you feel on Sunday early evening (talking about the Monday blues creeping in). Or think about your mood the previous evening just before you are about to go out with your friends for a trek, and then think about that time when the holiday is just about to get over. You got it! We always have our future on our minds.

Of course, it is important to think about the future but the focus should be on what you are doing right now. Enjoy the moment, be where you are currently with full awareness. Ensure that you have a great present so that your future is better by default.

As much as the mind puts you into your past, it is very well capable of creating an unrealistic future that has not existed, and mostly it gets into a negative thought process.

Thinking is a good exercise, however, it needs to be done in moderation. A healthy thought can build a healthy mind and can lead you to favorable action.

You should definitely plan and know what your goal is but once you know your goal, concentrate on your present until you reach where you want to. Yes, time and again you do need to monitor and analyse how far you've reached.

No one knows what the future is gonna hold. If we all had superpowers to decode that, life wouldn't be a fun game.

You don't like to watch a match when you know which team is winning right? Same thing ;)

88. Do you know your path finder?

Everyone has a unique story and has their set of experiences in their journey. If you look closely, you are actually playing your part without realizing you are also a part of someone else's story. In short, lives are interlinked.

Imagine your life without some of the closest people, also, think if they can imagine their lives without you. The answer would be rather difficult to think and we barely want to comprehend our otherwise simple but complex journeys.

Sometimes, unknowingly, some people become an integral part of our life and change everything around us and few small instances become an absolute game-changer that brings us to a totally new view. The point is, are we living without judging and questioning these bits and pieces that are a part of our path.

And most of all are we less grateful?! Think about it, even if you don't like something that happened to you in the past it may be because of that instance that you are here today. This changed self would have been completely different if you had not been through that bitter experience.

We are constantly guided to find our respective paths to get closer to our purpose, some of them may take longer to reach where they are supposed to, but everyone around us is your pathfinder. Everyone has helped you in some way or the other in getting closer to where you want to be. Never underestimate the master plan.

If you are going through a patch in your life which you think is not great enough for you to manage alone. Don't worry because someone already has your back and will take you through this.

Your journey is a collective effort of everyone who is unknowingly guiding you. You learn from situations and people and grow to be better than you were yesterday. #happylife

89. Procrastination is a Disease

Often, do you wonder what goes through your mind when you procrastinate? When you procrastinate over following something or getting something done or committing to a task, you are constantly focusing on not wanting to do the task and there is a reason why you do so.

Ever tried to find out the reason?

There is always a reason why you do something and why you don't do something. Something that you love doing, you will certainly find time to do despite your busy schedule. And, that something which you just hate or are lazy about you will find excuses of not getting it done.

In short, procrastination is a "larger term" for finding excuses, for not doing something. If you get rid of the excuses you get rid of delay and make peace with yourself to get things done. So what changed?

There is no magic to the word awareness, you must be aware constantly of your thoughts and your actions. The moment you are aware, you are in total control of what needs to be done. Once you are aware the second most important thing is to act. However, before actioning something you need to find out the reason for procrastinating it all this while.

Everyone gets a chance, but only a few make a choice of taking the risk and implementing with full commitment. If you look at successful people, you will notice that all of them are doers; they do what they plan and with consistent effort and commitment.

Procrastination will keep you away from your goal, you need to break that circle to be able to get where you want to be. Only your mind and the quality of your thoughts will decide your focus. you decide whether you want to focus on excuses or your purpose.

90. Watch when you think

Have you ever watched yourself think? Thinking is very involuntary sometimes and most of the time one gets consumed in the thoughts not aware of where it's taking them. However, what you think in your deep thoughts is what matters the most, it brings out the kind of person one is. The outer world may not know this side of your thought process because it is only for you.

However, there is no harm in analysing what kind of thought captivate your mind and gets you all the time which keeps you away from what is happening in your surroundings. I personally love this space of personal thinking, it's amazing what thoughts can do, and for me I keep motivated in my thoughts so that I have a positive outlook in real all the time. However, this is not what how I was always, over the period I have often watched my thoughts and directed a not so positive thought into a positive one.

When one practices and trains the mind to think in a direction the mind automatically starts moving the thoughts accordingly. It's amazing how mind functions.

These thoughts sometimes are also self-talks. Self-talks are often related to the way you want things to change, the way you reacted or the way you feel someone is and sometimes these are thoughts which are telling you to behave in a certain way with certain people.

The point here is we often behave in a way which is rather appreciated by others, there are very few who speak their mind and most of the times such people are tagged as "RUDE". If everyone starts speaking their mind without the filters it may get a bit uncomfortable. Also, the reason why one tends to have such a behaviour because we only look at things with our perspective, if we accept people the way they are then it would be much easier for us to comprehend the reason behind their thought process.

Our thoughts would then revolve around more relevant things. If each focuses on becoming better, we would have so much to learn from each other.

Our mind is a natural wonderer, let it wonder to place where we are happy visiting

91. It doesn't take much to change your life!

All the instances that have happened in your life had just witnessed a small instance and boom before you notice your life changed 360 degrees. Life is so simple yet so complex.

If you can think about one thing that happened in your life that changed something massive what would that instance be? Have you ever looked back to see what made your life take a turn? There are so many turns in our life that happen, some we know, and some happen without us realizing.

But this is one part of change where we don't have our control on, however we totally have control on ourselves the way we progress, the choices we make. Our decisions are a part of change; the decisions we have taken over a period have somehow led us to where we currently belong.

Most of us are procrastinating on something or the other. Some are waiting for the right time to start something new; some are trying to find a right time for working on themselves, but no one is realizing that in trying to find time they are missing on the "Now". Years later when one wakes up to a regret of not being able to do something is a bigger pain.

Realising the importance of a moment when it's gone is inutile

When one knows what needs to change that change should happen now. We all are wanting to get somewhere but if I ask you this question, you wouldn't have a specific answer. You know why?

Because you don't have a **WHY**

Everything we do is associated with a reason, and if you don't have a strong reason to justify what you are currently doing, you may have put yourself into a never-ending routine.

Always ask yourself why you are doing what you doing and if there is a better way. And, if you find a better way start working on it bit by bit.

We all are here for a purpose, find your purpose before your time is gone.

92. Our wrong behaviour sometimes feels right?

We tend to be immune to other people's opinion or likeability. Most of the times we feel that the way we behave is always right and we do not wish to step into other person's shoes before we declare them wrong.

It is difficult however to behave the way others want you to, but it is not that difficult to keep a self-check on our behaviour. Everyone is different and therefore carries a different perspective of how one views things and people around. Sometimes we are so much focused on how we should feel we forget how we are making others feel by our responses and reactions.

Only 10 percent fights happen due to difference in opinion rest 90 percent take place because of the tone in the voice. We don't really pay much attention to the way we are, but we always feel bad the way others react, this is just because we won't like to think that we may be reacting wrongly. And that, somewhere it is a part of our ego and ignorance.

Ohh yes it's difficult to accept that we have an ego but I think we moreover need to be aware of it rather than accepting it. Once we have a proof of instances it won't be difficult to accept.

Also, people tend to react instantly because it is the immediate reflex of the mind. Our mind requires practice and consistent training to be able to react in a composed manner.

Yes, it does get difficult sometimes to accept that we are wrong, however only a strong and mature mind will observe things as is. And it definitely takes a lot of practice to become strong headed. Only if you look at it neutrally would you be able to see why others reacted differently than you did.

The best thing about being wrong is you get to learn what you didn't know before.

Hope this book helps you think first and think twice about yourself because self focus should be our priority

My purpose of writing this book will be achieved even if this book helps one person identify with the thought process and change something for better.

Would love to hear your experience of this book, do write to me on my Instagram: silentlynoisy_